The Small Business Library

Incorporate Your Business:

The National Corporation Kit

1st Edition

by Daniel Sitarz
Attorney-at-Law

Nova Publishing Company
Small Business and Legal Publications
Carbondale, Illinois

Editorial and research assistance by Janet Harris Sitarz.

Cover design by Christine Jacquot of Spectrum Graphics, Murphysboro, IL.

Manufactured in the United States.

ISBN 0-935755-09-8

Library of Congress Catalog Card Number 94-45228

Library of Congress Cataloging-in-Publication Data
    Sitarz, Dan, 1948-
    Incorporate Your Business: the national corporation kit / by Daniel Sitarz - 1st ed.
    256 p. cm. (Small Business Library Series)
    includes index;
    ISBN 0-935755-09-8 : $18.95
    1. Incorporation--United States--Popular works. 2. Articles of Incorporation--United States--Popular works. I. Title. II. Series
    KF1420.Z9S58 1995   346.73'06622--dc20   [347.3066622] 94-45228   CIP

Nova Publishing Company is dedicated to providing up-to-date and accurate legal information to the public. All Nova publications are periodically revised to contain the latest available legal information.

1st Edition; 1st Printing: September, 1995

This publication is designed to provide accurate and authoritative information in regard to the subject matter covered. It is sold with the understanding that the publisher and author are not engaged in rendering legal, accounting, or other professional services. If legal advice or other expert assistance is required, the services of a competent professional person should be sought.

*From a Declaration of Principles jointly adopted by a Committee of
the American Bar Association and a Committee of Publishers*

DISCLAIMER

Because of possible unanticipated changes in governing statutes and case law relating to the application of any information contained in this book, the author, publisher, and any and all persons or entities involved in any way in the preparation, publication, sale, or distribution of this book disclaim all responsibility for the legal effects or consequences of any document prepared or action taken in reliance upon information contained in this book. No representations, either express or implied, are made or given regarding the legal consequences of the use of any information contained in this book. Purchasers and persons intending to use this book for the preparation of any legal documents are advised to check specifically on the current applicable laws in any jurisdiction in which they intend the documents to be effective. This book is not printed, published, sold, circulated, or distributed with the intention that it be used to procure or aid in the procurement of any legal effect or ruling in any jurisdiction in which such procurement or aid may be restricted by statute.

Nova Publishing Company
Legal Publications
1103 West College Street
Carbondale IL 62901
1(800)748-1175

Distributed to the trade by:
National Book Network
4720 Boston Way
Lanham MD 20706
1(800)462-6420

Table of Contents

CHAPTER 10: Corporate Resolutions 140

CHAPTER 11: Corporate Stock 175

Preface

This book is part of Nova Publishing Company's continuing Small Business Library series. The various business guides in this series are prepared by business professionals who feel that small business owners deserve the clearest and most understandable information available to assist them in running their businesses. The various business references in this series are designed to provide concrete information to small business owners to allow them to understand and operate their own businesses with a minimum of outside assistance.

With the proper information, the average person in today's world can easily understand and operate a small business and apply many areas of law. However, each year many thousands of small businesses fail because their owners have been unable to manage their financial, legal, or management affairs properly. This book and others in Nova's Small Business Library series are intended to provide the necessary information to those members of the public who wish to both understand and operate their own businesses.

However, in an area as complex as corporate law, it is not always prudent to attempt to handle every legal situation which arises without the aid of a competent attorney. Although the information presented in this book will give readers a basic understanding of the areas of law covered, it is not intended that this text entirely substitute for experienced legal assistance in all situations. Throughout this book there are references to those particular situations in which the aid of a lawyer or other professional is strongly recommended.

Regardless of whether or not a lawyer is ultimately retained in certain situations, the legal information in this handbook will enable the reader to understand the framework of corporate law in this country and how to effectively use legal forms in the operation of their business corporation.

To try and make that task as easy as possible, technical legal jargon has been eliminated whenever possible and plain English used instead. Naturally, plain and easily-understood English is not only perfectly proper for use in all legal documents but, in most cases, leads to far less confusion on the part of later readers. When it is necessary in this book to use a legal term which may be unfamiliar to most people, the word will be shown in *italics* and defined when first used. A glossary of legal terms most often encountered in corporate legal documents is included at the end of this book.

Chapter 1

Deciding to Form a Corporation

One of the first decisions that a potential business owner must confront is how their business should be structured and operated. This crucial decision must be made even before the business has actually begun operations. The legal documents which will generally accompany the formation of a business can follow many different patterns, depending on the particular situation and the type of business to be undertaken.

Initially, the type of business entity to be used must be selected. There are many basic forms of business operating entities. The five most common forms are:

- Sole proprietorship,
- Standard partnership,
- Limited partnership,
- Standard corporation,
- "S" corporation.

The choice of entity for a particular business depends on many factors. Which of these forms of business organization is chosen can have a great impact on the success of the business. The structure chosen will have an effect on how easy it is to obtain financing, how taxes are paid, how accounting records are kept, whether personal assets are at risk in the venture, the amount of control the "owner" has over the business, and many other aspects of the business. Keep in mind that the initial choice of business organization need not be the final choice. It is often wise to begin with the simplest form, the sole proprietorship, until the business progresses to a point where another form is clearly indicated. This allows the business to begin in the least complicated manner and allows the owner to retain total control in the important formative period of the business. As the business grows and the potential for liability and tax burdens increase, circumstances may dictate a re-examination of the business structure. The advantages and disadvantages of the five choices of business operation are detailed below.

The Sole Proprietorship

A sole proprietorship is both the simplest and the most prevalent form of business organization. An important reason for this is that it is the least regulated of all types of business structures. Technically, the *sole proprietorship* is the traditional unincorporated one-person business. For legal and tax purposes, the business is the owner. It has no existence outside the owner. The liabilities of the business are personal to the owner and the business ends when the owner dies. On the other hand, all of the profits are also personal to the owner and the sole owner has full control of the business.

Disadvantages

Perhaps the most important factor to consider before choosing this type of business structure is that all of the personal and business assets of the sole owner are at risk in the sole proprietorship. If the demands of the creditors of the business exceed those assets which were formally placed in the name of the business, the creditors may reach the personal assets of the owner of the sole proprietorship. Legal judgements for damages arising from the operation of the business may also be enforced against the owner's personal assets. This unlimited liability is probably the greatest drawback to this type of business form. Of course, insurance coverage of various types can lessen the dangers inherent in having one's personal assets at risk in a business. However, as liability insurance premiums continue to skyrocket, it is unlikely that a fledgling small business can afford to insure against all manner of contingencies and at the maximum coverage levels necessary to guard against all risk to personal assets.

A second major disadvantage to the sole proprietorship as a form of business structure is the potential difficulty in obtaining business loans. Often in starting a small business, there is insufficient collateral to obtain a loan and the sole owner must mortgage his or her own house or other personal assets to obtain the loan. This, of course, puts the sole proprietor's personal assets in a direct position of risk should the business fail. Banks and other lending institutions are often reluctant to loan money for initial small business start-ups due to the high risk of failure for small businesses. Without a proven track record, it is quite difficult for a small business owner to adequately present a loan proposal based on a sufficiently stable cash flow to satisfy most banks.

A further disadvantage to a sole proprietorship is the lack of continuity which is inherent in the business form. If the owner dies, the business ceases to exist. Of course, the assets and liabilities of the business will pass to the heirs of the owner, but the expertise and knowledge of how the business was successfully carried on will often die with the owner. Small sole proprietorships are seldom carried on profitably after the death of the owner.

Advantages

The most appealing advantage of the sole proprietorship as a business structure is the total control the owner has over the business. Subject only to economic considerations and certain legal restrictions, there is total freedom to operate the business however one chooses. Many people feel that this factor alone is enough to overcome the inherent disadvantages in this form of business.

Related to this is the simplicity of organization of the sole proprietorship. Other than maintenance of sufficient records for tax purposes, there are no legal requirements on how the business is operated. Of course, the prudent business-person will keep adequate records and sufficiently organize the business for its most efficient operation. But there are no outside forces dictating how such internal decisions are made in the sole proprietorship. The sole owner makes all decisions in this type of business.

As was mentioned earlier, the sole proprietorship is the least regulated of all businesses. Normally, the only license necessary is a local business license, usually obtained by simply paying a fee to a local registration authority. In addition, it may be necessary to file an affidavit with local authorities and publish a notice in a local newspaper if the business is operated under an assumed or fictitious name. This is necessary to allow creditors to have access to the actual identity of the true owner of the business, since it is the owner who will be personally liable for the debts and obligations of the business.

Finally, it may be necessary to register with local, state, and federal tax bodies for I.D. numbers and for the purpose of collection of sales and other taxes. Other than these few simple registrations, from a legal standpoint little else is required to start up a business as a sole proprietorship.

A final and important advantage to the sole proprietorship is the various tax benefits available to an individual. The losses or profits of the sole proprietorship are considered personal to the owner. The losses are directly deductible against any other income the owner may have and the profits are taxed only once at the marginal rate of the owner. In many instances, this may have distinct advantages over the method by which partnerships are taxed or the double taxation of corporations, particularly in the early stages of the business.

The Partnership

A *partnership* is a relationship existing between two or more persons who join together to carry on a trade or business. Each partner contributes money, property, labor, or skill to the partnership and, in return, expects to share in the profits or losses of the business. A partnership is usually based on a partnership agreement of some type, although the agreement need not be a formal document. It may even simply be an oral understanding between the partners, although this is not recommended.

A simple joint undertaking to share expenses is not considered a partnership, nor is a mere co-ownership of property that is maintained and leased or rented. To be considered a partnership for legal and tax purposes, the following factors are usually considered:

- The partner's conduct in carrying out the provisions of the partnership agreement;
- The relationship of the parties;
- The abilities and contributions of each party to the partnership;
- The control each partner has over the partnership income and the purposes for which the income is used.

Disadvantages

The disadvantages to the partnership form of business begin with the potential for conflict between the partners. Of all forms of business organization, the partnership has spawned more disagreements than any other. This is generally traceable to the lack of a decisive initial partnership agreement which clearly outlines the rights and duties of the partners. This disadvantage can be partially overcome with a comprehensive partnership agreement. However, there is still the seemingly inherent difficulty that many people have in working within the framework of a partnership, regardless of the initial agreement between the partners.

A further disadvantage to the partnership structure is that each partner is subject to unlimited personal liability for the debts of the partnership. The potential liability in a partnership is even greater than that encountered in a sole proprietorship. This is due to the fact that in a partnership the personal risk for which one may be liable is partially out of one's direct control and may be accrued due to actions on the part of another person. Each partner is liable for all of the debts of the partnership, regardless of which of the partners may have been responsible for their accumulation.

Related to the business risks of personal financial liability is the potential personal legal liability for the negligence of another partner. In addition, each partner may even be liable for the negligence of an employee of the partnership if such negligence takes place during the usual course of business of the partnership. Again, the attendant risks are broadened by the potential for liability based on the acts of other persons. Of course, general liability insurance can counteract this drawback to some extent to protect the personal and partnership assets of each partner.

Again, as with the sole proprietorship, the partnership lacks the advantage of continuity. A partnership is usually automatically terminated upon the death of any partner. A final accounting and a division of assets and liabilities is generally necessary in such an instance unless specific methods under which the partnership may be continued have been outlined in the partnership agreement.

Finally, certain benefits of corporate organization are not available to a partnership. Since a partnership can not obtain financing through public stock offerings, large infusions of capital are more difficult for a partnership to raise than for a corporation. In addition, many of the fringe benefit programs that are available to corporations (such as certain pension and profit-sharing arrangements) are not available to partnerships.

Advantages

A partnership, by virtue of combining the credit potential of the various partners, has an inherently greater opportunity for business credit than is generally available to a sole proprietorship. In addition, the assets which are placed in the name of the partnership may often be used directly as collateral for business loans. The pooling of the personal capital of the partners generally provides the partnership with an advantage over the sole-proprietorship in the area of cash availability. However, as noted above, the partnership does not have as great a potential for financing as does a corporation.

As with the sole proprietorship, there may be certain tax advantages to operation of a business as a partnership, as opposed to a corporation. The profits generated by a partnership may be distributed directly to the partners without incurring any "double" tax liability, as is the case with the distribution of corporate profits in the form of dividends to the shareholders. Income from a partnership is taxed at personal income tax rates. Note, however, that depending on the individual tax situation of each partner, this aspect could prove to be a disadvantage.

For a business in which two or more people desire to share in the work and in the profits, a partnership is often the structure chosen. It is, potentially, a much simpler form of business organization than the corporate form. Less start-up costs are necessary and there is limited regulation of partnerships. However, the simplicity of this form of business can be deceiving. A sole proprietor knows that his or her actions will determine how the business will prosper, and that he or she is, ultimately, personally responsible for the success or failure of the enterprise. In a partnership, however, the duties, obligations and commitments of each partner are often ill-defined. This lack of definition of the status of each partner can lead to serious difficulties and disagreements. In order to clarify the rights and responsibilities of each partner and to be certain of the tax status of the partnership, it is good business procedure to have a written partnership agreement. All states have adopted a version of the Uniform Partnership Act. Although state law will supply the general boundaries of partnerships and even specific partnership agreement terms if they are not addressed by a written partnership agreement, it is more conducive to a clear understanding of the business structure if the partner's agreements are put in writing.

The Limited Partnership

The *limited partnership* is a hybrid type of business structure. It contains elements of both a traditional partnership and a corporation. The limited partnership form of business structure may be used when some interested parties desire to invest in a partnership but also desire to have limited liability and exercise no control over the partnership management. Limited partnerships are, generally, a more complex form of business operation than either the sole proprietorship or the standard partnership.

Limited partnerships are also subject to far more state regulations regarding both their formation and operation. All states have adopted a version of the Uniform Limited Partnership Act. If the limited partnership form of business is chosen, the services of a competent business attorney should be used for drawing up the proper documents.

A limited partnership consists of one or more general partners who actively manage the business of the partnership and one or more limited partners who are mere investors in the partnership and who have no active role in the management of the partnership. A general partner is treated much as a partner in a traditional partnership, while a limited partner is treated much as a shareholder in a corporation. The general partners are at personal risk in a limited partnership. The limited partners enjoy a limited liability equal to their investment as long as they do not actively engage in any management of the partnership.

Disadvantages

In as much as the business form is still a partnership, there is still a potential for conflict among the partners. This potential is somewhat mitigated in the limited partnership by the distancing of the limited partners from the actual management of the partnership. If the passive limited partners engage in any efforts to exert control over the management, they risk losing the benefits of limited liability that they enjoy.

Limited partnerships are formed according to individual state law, generally by filing formal Articles of Limited Partnership with the proper state authorities in the state of formation. They are subject to more paperwork requirements than a simple partnership.

Similar to traditional partnerships, the limited partnership has an inherent lack of continuity. This may, however, be overcome in the case of the retirement or death of a general partner by providing in the Articles of Limited Partnership for an immediate reorganization of the limited partnership with the retired partner eliminated or the deceased partner's heirs or estate becoming a limited partner.

Advantages

The limited partners in such a business enjoy a limited liability, similar to that of a shareholder in a corporation. Their risk is limited to the amount of their investment in the limited partnership. The general partners remain at full personal risk, the same as a partner in a traditional partnership.

Since the limited partners will have no personal liability and will not be required to personally perform any tasks of management, it is easier to attract investors to the limited partnership form of business than to a traditional partnership. The limited partner will share in the potential profits and in the tax deductions of the limited partnership, but in fewer of the financial risks involved.

The Corporation

Corporations are the focus of this book. A corporation is a creation of law. It is governed by the laws of the state of incorporation and of the state or states in which it does business. In recent years it has become the business structure of choice for many small businesses. Corporations are, generally, a more complex form of business operation than either a sole proprietorship or partnership. They are also subject to far more state regulations regarding both their formation and operation. The following discussion is provided in order to allow the potential business owner an understanding of this type of business operation.

The *corporation* is an artificial entity. It is created by filing *Articles of Incorporation* with the proper state authorities. This gives the corporation its legal existence and the right to carry on business. The Articles of Incorporation act as a public record of certain formalities of corporate existence. Preparation of Articles of Incorporation is explained in detail in Chapter 5. Adoption of corporate *By-Laws*, or internal rules of operation, is often the first business of the corporation, after it has been given the authority to conduct business by the state. The By-Laws of the corporation outline the actual mechanics of the operation and management of the corporation. The preparation of corporate By-Laws is explained in Chapter 6.

In its simplest form, the corporate organizational structure consists of the following levels:

- Shareholders: who own shares of the business but do not contribute to the direct management of the corporation, other than by electing the directors of the corporation, and voting on major corporate issues.

- Directors: who may be shareholders, but as directors do not own any of the business. They are responsible, jointly as members of the *board of directors* of the corporation, for making the major business decisions of the corporation, including appointing the officers of the corporation.

- Officers: who may be shareholders and/or directors, but, as officers, do not own any of the business. The officers (generally the president, vice president, secretary, and treasurer) are responsible for the day-to-day operation of the corporate business.

Disadvantages

Due to the nature of the organizational structure in a corporation, a certain degree of individual control is necessarily lost by incorporation. The officers, as appointees of the board of directors, are answerable to the board for management decisions. The board of directors, on the other hand, is not entirely free from restraint, since they are responsible to the shareholders for the prudent business management of the corporation.

The technical formalities of corporation formation and operation must be strictly observed in order for a business to reap the benefits of corporate existence. For this reason, there is an additional burden and expense to the corporation of detailed record keeping that is seldom present in other forms of business organization. Corporate decisions are, in general, more complicated due to the various levels of control and all such decisions must be carefully documented. Corporate meetings, both at the shareholder and director levels, are more formal and more frequent. In addition, the actual formation of the corporation is more expensive than the formation of either a sole proprietorship or partnership. The initial state fees that must be paid for registration of a corporation with a state can run as high as $900.00 for a minimally-capitalized corporation. Corporations are also subject to a greater level of governmental regulation than any other type of business entity. These complications have the potential to overburden a small business struggling to survive. The forms and instructions in this book are all designed to lessen the burden and expense of operating a business corporation.

Finally, the profits of a corporation, when distributed to the shareholders in the form of dividends, are subject to being taxed twice. The first tax comes at the corporate level. The distribution of any corporate profits to the investors in the form of dividends is not a deductible business expense for the corporation. Thus, any dividends which are distributed to shareholders have already been subject to corporate income tax. The second level of tax is imposed at the personal level. The receipt of corporate dividends is considered income to the individual shareholder and is taxed as such. This potential for higher taxes due to a corporate business structure can be moderated by many factors however. Forms dealing with taxation of corporations are contained in Chapter 14.

Advantages

One of the most important advantages to the corporate form of business structure is the potential limited liability of the founders of and investors in the corporation. The liability for corporate debts is limited, in general, to the amount of money each owner has contributed to the corporation. Unless the corporation is essentially a shell for a one-person business or unless the corporation is grossly under-capitalized or under-insured, the personal assets of the owners are not at risk if the corporation fails. The shareholders stand to lose only what they invested. This factor is very important in attracting investors as the business grows.

A corporation can have a perpetual existence. Theoretically, a corporation can last forever. This may be a great advantage if there are potential future changes in ownership of the business in the offing. Changes that would cause a partnership to be dissolved or terminated often will not affect the corporation. This continuity can be an important factor in establishing a stable business image and a permanent relationship with others in the industry.

Unlike a partnership, in which no one may become a partner without the consent of the other partners, a shareholder of corporate stock may freely sell, trade, or give away their stock unless this right is formally restricted by reasonable corporate decisions. The new owner of such stock is then a new owner of the business in the proportionate share of stock obtained. This freedom offers potential investors a liquidity to shift assets that is not present in the partnership form of business. The sale of shares by the corporation is also an attractive method by which to raise needed capital. The sale of shares of a corporation, however, is subject to many governmental regulations, on both the state and federal levels.

Taxation is listed both as an advantage and as a disadvantage for the corporation. Depending on many factors, the use of a corporation can increase or decrease the actual income tax paid in operating a corporate business. In addition, corporations may set aside surplus earnings (up to certain levels) without any negative tax consequences. Finally, corporations are able to offer a much greater variety of fringe benefit programs to employees and officers than any other type of business entity. Various retirement, stock option, and profit-sharing plans are only open to corporate participation.

The "S" Corporation

The *"S" corporation* is a certain type of corporation that is available for specific tax purposes. It is a creature of the Internal Revenue Service. "S" corporation status is not relevant to state corporation laws. Its purpose is to allow small corporations to choose to be taxed, at the federal level, like a partnership, but to also enjoy many of the benefits of a corporation. The details of obtaining "S" corporation status are contained in Chapter 13.

In general, to qualify as an "S" corporation under current IRS rules, a corporation meet certain requirements:

- It must not have over 35 shareholders;
- All of the shareholders must be individuals;
- It must only have one class of stock;
- Shareholders must consent to "S" corporation status; and
- An election of "S" corporation status must be filed with the IRS.

The "S" corporation retains all of the advantages and disadvantages of the traditional corporation except in the area of taxation. For tax purposes, "S" corporation shareholders are treated similarly to partners in a partnership. The income, losses, and deductions generated by an "S" corporation are "passed through" the corporate entity to the individual shareholders. Thus, there is no "double" taxation of an "S"-type corporation. In addition, unlike a standard corporation, shareholders of "S" corporations can personally deduct any corporate losses.

The decision of which business entity to choose depends upon many factors and should be carefully studied. If the choice is to operate a business as a corporation or "S" corporation, this book will provide an array of easy-to-use legal forms which will, in most cases, allow the business owner to start and operate the corporation with minimal difficulty while meeting all of the legal paperwork requirements.

Chapter 2

Operating a Corporation

The corporate business structure has three levels: shareholders, directors, and officers. In order to understand the requirements for corporate record-keeping, it is necessary to understand how a corporation actually functions. Each level has different rights and different responsibilities. Each level also generates different types of paperwork. Although all three levels of corporate management may often work together and may even be the same individual, they must be treated as separate parts of the corporate structure.

Shareholders

The shareholders are the persons or other business entities who actually own the corporation. The corporation ownership is divided into shares of stock in the corporation. Each share may be then sold to shareholders who are then issued a stock certificate which represents their ownership of a percentage of the corporation, represented by numbers of shares of stock. Although many different levels and classes of stock ownership may be designated, the forms and discussions in this book will deal with only one class of stock: common stock. Each share of stock is, generally, afforded one vote in shareholder decisions. Although it is perfectly acceptable to provide for non-voting classes of stock, the forms and discussion in this book will only relate to voting shares of stock.

The ownership of stock certificates of the corporation is recorded in the corporate *stock transfer book*. This "book" can simply consist of a few pages in the corporate record book with places to note the issuance and transfer of certificates. Stock and stock transfer records are detailed in Chapter 11. The corporate record book which will contain all of the corporate records (except the accounting records) can consist of a simple 3-ring binder in which the records are organized. It is possible to purchase fancy corporate record books, but they are not a legal requirement.

Ownership of shares of stock in a corporation brings with it both benefits and responsibilities. The benefits stem from the right to a share of ownership in the assets of the corporation. The business profits of the corporation may also be shared with the shareholders in the form of dividends. The decision of the corporation to issue dividends on stock, however, is within the realm of the board of directors. The main responsibility of the shareholders is to elect the directors of the corporation. The shareholders also have authority to vote on extraordinary business actions of the corporation. These actions are generally limited to decisive activities of the corporation, such as the sale of all of the assets of the corporation, the merger of the corporation, or the dissolution of the corporation. Shareholders, finally, also generally have the right to approve any amendments to the Articles of Incorporation. Shareholders authority to direct the business only comes from the right to undertake these few actions. Their power must also always be exercised as a group. An individual shareholder has no power to direct the management of the corporation in any way, other than to buy or sell shares of stock.

The election of the directors of the corporation takes place at the annual meeting of the shareholders, although directors can be elected for terms which last for more than one year. At the annual meeting, the president and treasurer of the corporation (both officers of the corporation) will present their annual reports on the activities and financial state of the corporation. The shareholders will then elect (generally by secret ballot majority vote) the directors for the following year. If there are any major business decisions, these may also be addressed. The minutes of this meeting and any shareholders resolutions are typically the only shareholder records to be maintained, other than the stock transfer book. Shareholders meetings and paperwork are generally contained in Chapter 9. Specific shareholder resolutions regarding amendments to Articles of Incorporation and By-Laws and "S" corporation status are contained in Chapters 7 and 13, respectively. Shareholders may also choose to enter into various shareholders agreements regarding their stock rights or voting privileges. Shareholders agreements are explained in Chapter 12.

Directors

As explained, the directors are elected by the shareholders at their annual meetings. Please note, however, that in the forms contained in this book, the initial board of directors is specified in the Articles of Incorporation which are prepared and filed with the state. This is to comply with many state's statutes which require this. The directors which are selected in the Articles may then be approved by the shareholders at their first meeting or may be rejected and new directors elected.

The directors of the corporation must act as members of the board of directors. Individual directors, acting alone, have no authority to bind the corporation or, for example, to enter into contracts or leases for the corporation. The directors must act as a board of directors. Most states, however, allow corporations to have only a single director. This sole director must, however, continue to act as a board of directors. Please check the Appendix for the specific requirements in your state. The board of directors of a corporation has two main responsibilities. The first is to appoint and oversee the officers who will handle the day-to-day actions of actually running the business. The second responsibility is for setting out the corporate policies and making most major decisions on corporate financial and business matters. The policies of the corporation are first contained in the corporate By-Laws which will be prepared by the board of directors. Subsequent corporate policies can be outlined in board of director's resolutions, unless they conflict with the By-Laws. In such a case, the By-Laws must be formally amended by the board of directors, with the consent and approval of the shareholders. Thus, it is the directors who have the actual central authority and responsibility in a corporation.

This differentiation of responsibilities in corporate management is crucial and often difficult to grasp. The shareholders only have the right elect the directors and to vote on major extraordinary business of the corporation (merger, complete sale of the corporation, dissolution, or amendments of the Articles of Incorporation). The director's role is much wider. They have the power to authorize the corporation to enter into contracts, to purchase property, to open bank accounts, to borrow or loan money, and other such significant actions. The board can also delegate this authority to its officers, but—and this is crucial—it must do so in writing with a specific board of directors resolution. In many corporations, in fact, much of the actual operations are handled by the officers. However, all of the officer's authority to operate on behalf of the corporation stems directly from the board of directors.

The bulk of the records of the corporation will consist of matters within the province of the board of directors. The directors will hold annual meetings for the purpose of appointing corporate officers and conducting any other business.

They may also hold, with proper notice, special meetings to transact other corporate business which may develop from time to time. The minutes of all directors meetings are very important in establishing that a separate corporate entity has been respected by the persons involved with the corporate management. These minutes must be detailed, complete and must be kept up to date. The various actions of the directors must be documented in formal resolutions. These resolutions are often required by banks and other businesses with which the corporation does business in order to verify that the corporation has authorized the particular transaction. The details of directors meetings and resolutions are outlined in Chapters 8 and 10. Directors resolutions regarding amendments to the Articles of Incorporation and By-Laws are included in Chapter 7. It should be noted that a few states have chosen to allow the shareholders of a corporation to actively participate in the management of the corporation. Although this may allow for ease of management in certain instances, it will not lessen the requirement for corporate record-keeping. The forms in this book are all designed for use in traditional three-tiered corporate management: shareholders, directors, and officers.

Officers

To the officers of a corporation falls the responsibilities of running the business. Their powers, however, are dictated solely by the board of directors. They can be given very broad powers to transact virtually all business for the corporation, or they can be tightly limited in their authority. A single shareholder can act as both the sole director and the sole officer of a corporation in most states. The officers, however, even in this circumstance, still derive their authority from resolutions of the board of directors. Prudent businesses often require copies of the authorizing resolutions in the course of large transactions.

There may be many levels of corporate officers. Traditionally, there are four main officers: president, vice-president, treasurer, and secretary. Their specific powers should be outlined by the directors in the corporate By-Laws and their authority to transact individual business deals should be detailed in board of director's resolutions. In general, the president acts as the corporation's general manager, handling the day-to-day operations. The vice-president normally acts only in the absence of the president, although this officer can be given specific responsibilities. The treasurer handles the corporate funds and is responsible for the accounting books. The secretary handles the corporate records (minutes, resolutions, etc.) and is also generally responsible for the corporate stock and stock transfer book.

The officers are appointed by the board of directors at annual meetings, although special meetings can be called for this purpose. The officers may be required to report individually to the board. Often the president will be called upon to present an annual report regarding the overall condition of the corporation. The treasurer will present an annual financial report at the directors meeting. The secretary will handle all of the records, including copies of these annual reports. In many corporations, the president keeps in contact with the board of directors on a much more continual basis. However, any major decisions which affect the corporation should be carefully documented and, if necessary, a special meeting of the board of directors should be called and a formal resolution adopted.

The formalities of corporate structure may seem complex for small businesses and even foolish for corporations with a single owner/director/officer. It is important to understand that it is the recognition of this structure and the documentation of corporate actions taken within this structure which afford the corporation with its limited liability protection and taxation benefits. The specific formalities for preparing Articles of Incorporation are contained in Chapter 5; for adopting By-Laws, Chapter 6; for Directors meetings, Chapter 8; and for Shareholders meetings, Chapter 9.

Chapter 3

Corporate Paperwork

The business arena in America operates on a daily assortment of legal forms. There are more legal forms in use in American business than are used in the operations and government of many foreign countries. The business corporation is not immune to this flood of legal forms. Indeed the operation of a corporation, in general, requires more legal documents than does any other form of business. While large corporations are able to obtain and pay expensive lawyers to deal with their legal problems and paperwork, most small businesses can not afford such a course of action. The small business corporation must deal with a variety of legal documents, usually without the aid of an attorney.

Unfortunately, many business people who are confronted with such forms do not understand the legal ramifications of the use of these forms. They simply sign them with the expectation that it is a fairly standard document, without any unusual legal provisions. They trust that the details of the particular document will fall within what is generally accepted within the industry or trade. In most cases, this may be true. In many situations, however, it is not. Our court system is clogged with cases in which two businesses are battling over what was really intended by the incomprehensible legal language in a certain legal document.

Much of the confusion over corporate paperwork comes from two areas: First, there is a general lack of understanding among many in business regarding the framework of law. Second, many corporate documents are written in antiquated legal jargon that is difficult for even most lawyers to understand and nearly impossible for a lay person to comprehend.

The various legal documents that are used in this book are, however, written in plain English. Standard legal jargon, as used in most lawyer-prepared documents, is, for most people, totally incomprehensible. Despite the lofty arguments by attorneys regarding the need for such strained and difficult language, the vast majority of legalese is absolutely unnecessary. As with any form of communication, clarity, simplicity, and readability should be the goal in legal documents.

Unfortunately, in some specific instances, certain obscure legal terms are the only words that accurately and precisely describe some things in certain legal contexts. In those few cases, the unfamiliar legal term will be defined when first used. Generally, however, simple terms are used throughout this book. In most cases, masculine and feminine terms have been eliminated and the generic *it* or *them* used instead. In the few situations in which this leads to awkward sentence construction, *her/his* or *she/he* may be used instead.

All of the legal documents contained in this book have been prepared in essentially the same manner by which attorneys create legal forms. Many people believe that lawyers prepare each legal document that they compose entirely from scratch. Nothing could be further from the truth. Invariably, lawyers begin their preparation of a legal document with a standardized legal form book. Every law library has multi-volume sets of these encyclopedic texts which contain blank forms for virtually every conceivable legal situation. Armed with these preprepared legal forms, lawyers, in many cases, simply fill in the blanks and have their secretaries re-type the form for the client. Of course, the client is generally unaware of this process. As the lawyers begin to specialize in a certain area of legal expertise, they compile their own files containing such blank forms.

This book provides those business-persons who wish to form a corporation with a set of legal forms which has been prepared with the problems and normal legal requirements of the small business corporation in mind. They are intended to be used in those situations that are clearly described by their terms. Of course, while most corporate document use will fall within the bounds of standard business practices, some legal circumstances will present non-standard situations. The forms in this book are designed to be readily adaptable to most usual business situations. They may be carefully altered to conform to the particular transaction that confronts your business. However, if you are faced with a complex or tangled business situation, the advice of a competent lawyer is highly recommended. If you wish, you may also create forms for certain standard situations for your corporation and have your lawyer check them for any local legal circumstances.

The proper and cautious use of the forms provided in this book will allow the typical corporation to save considerable money on legal costs over the course of the life of the business, while enabling the business to comply with legal and governmental regulations. Perhaps more importantly, these forms will provide a method by which the business-person can avoid costly misunderstandings about what exactly was intended in a particular situation. By using the forms provided to clearly document the proceedings of everyday corporate operations, disputes over what was really meant can be avoided. This protection will allow the business to avoid many potential lawsuits and operate more efficiently in compliance with the law.

The Importance of Corporate Record-Keeping

The amount of paperwork and record-keeping required by the use of the corporate form of business may often seem overwhelming. Sometimes, it may even seem senseless. However, there are some very important reasons why detailed records of corporate operations are necessary. A corporation is a fiction. It is a creation of the government to enable businesses to have a flexibility to function in a complex national and even international marketplace. This form of enterprise provides the most adaptable type of business entity in today's world. Through the use of a corporate entity, a business may respond quickly to the changing nature of modern business. Of course, the limited liability of corporate investors is also a great advantage over other forms of business organization.

A corporation is, in many cases, afforded the legal status of a person. It may sue or be sued in its own name. A corporation may own property in its own name. In most situations, a corporation is treated as if it has a life of its own. In a legal sense, it does have a life of its own. It was born by filing the Articles of Incorporation with a state and it may die upon filing Articles of Dissolution with the state. While a corporation is *alive*, it is said to exist. During its existence, it can operate as a separate legal entity and enjoy the benefits of corporate status *as long as certain corporate formalities are observed*. The importance of following these basic corporate formalities can not be over-emphasized. All of the advantages of operating under the corporate form of business are directly dependent upon careful observance of a few basic paperwork and management requirements.

Each major action which a corporation undertakes must be carefully documented. Even if there are only a few, or even a single shareholder, complete records of corporate activities must be recorded. There must be minutes, records of shareholders meetings which outline the election of directors of the corporation. Directors meetings must also be documented and the actions of directors recorded in the form of resolutions. Stock certificates must be issued and the ownership of them must be carefully tracked. This is true regardless of the size of the corporation. In fact, as the size of the corporation decreases, the importance of careful record-keeping actually increases.

Corporate existence can be challenged in court. This will most likely happen in circumstances where a creditor of the corporation or victim of some corporate disaster is left without compensation, due to the limited liability of the corporation. Despite the fact that the corporation has been accepted by the state as a legal entity, if the formalities of corporate existence have not been carefully followed, the owners of a corporation are at risk. The court may decide that a single shareholder corporation merely used the corporation as a shell to avoid liability. The court is then empowered to *pierce the corporate veil* or declare that the corporation was actually merely the *alter ego* of the owner. In either outcome, the court can disregard the existence of the corporation and the creditors or victims can reach the personal assets of the owner. This most often will occur when a corporation is formed without sufficient capitalization to reasonably cover normal business affairs; when the corporation has not maintained sufficient insurance to cover standard contingencies; when the owner has mingled corporate funds with his/her own; and when there are no records to indicate that the corporation was actually operated as a separate entity. The results of such a lawsuit can be devastating. The loss of personal assets and the loss of corporate legal status for tax purposes can often lead to impoverishment and bankruptcy.

This difficulty is not a rarity. Each year, many corporations are found to be shams which were not operated as separate business entities. In a lawsuit against a small corporation, an attack on the use of corporate formalities is often the single most powerful weapon of the opposition. The best defense against an attack on the use of a corporate business form is to always have treated the corporation as a separate entity. This requires documenting each and every major business activity in minutes, records, and resolutions. When it is desired that the corporation undertake a particular activity, the directors should meet and adopt a resolution which clearly identifies the action and the reasons for the action. If major actions are undertaken, the shareholders may also need to meet and document their assent. This is true even if there is only one shareholder who is also the single director. With such records, it is an easy task to establish that the actions taken were done for the benefit of the corporation and not for the personal betterment of the individual owner or owners. As long as it can be clearly shown that the owners respected the corporate separateness, the corporate existence can not be disregarded by the courts, even if there is only one shareholder who is also the sole director and only officer of the corporation. It is not the size of the corporation, but rather the existence of complete corporate records which provides the protection from liability for the owners of the corporation. It is crucial to recognize this vital element in operating a corporation. Careful, detailed record-keeping is the key to enjoying the tax benefits and limited liability of the corporate business structure.

How Use To This Book

In each chapter of this book, you will find an introductory section that will give you an overview of the types of situations in which the forms or form clauses in that chapter will generally be used. Following that overview, there will be a brief explanation of the specific uses for each form. This explanation will, generally, include a listing of the information that must be compiled to complete the form.

The forms are not designed to be torn out of this book. It is expected that the forms may be used on more than one occasion. The preferable manner for using these forms is to make a photo-copy of the form, fill in the information that is necessary, and then re-type the form in its entirety on clean white letter sized paper. The trend in the legal profession is to move entirely to letter sized (8 1/2" X 11") paper. In fact, many court systems (including the entire Federal court system) now refuse to accept documents on legal sized paper.

> **Note For Computer Users**: All of the forms which are included in this book may be obtained on computer diskettes. Please see ordering information on the last page of this book.

It is recommended that you review the table of contents of this book in order to gain a broad overview of the range and type of legal documents that are available. Then, before you prepare any of the forms for use, you should carefully read the introductory information and instructions in the chapter in which the particular form is contained. Try to be as detailed and specific as possible as you fill in these forms. The more precise the description, the less likelihood that later disputes may develop over what was actually intended by the language chosen. The forms may be carefully adopted to a particular situation which may confront your corporation. However, be very careful in altering the Articles of Incorporation and corporate By-Laws. Certain clauses are mandatory in these documents and must be included.

The careful preparation and use of the legal forms in this book should provide the typical business corporation with most of the legal documents necessary for day-to-day operations. If in doubt as to whether a particular form will work in a specific application, please consult a competent lawyer. It may also be wise to consult with an experienced accountant as you begin to organize the corporation. The tax laws regarding corporations are very complex and must be carefully complied with in order to obtain the maximum tax benefits. Understanding the use of the corporate business entity and the use of corporate forms will enable you to intelligently discuss your corporation with the professionals which you choose to assist you in your business.

Corporate Paperwork Checklist

The following checklist outlines the various corporate documents which should be prepared and maintained during the life of a corporation:

☐ Pre-Incorporation Checklist (see Chapter 4)

☐ Reservation of corporate name (filed with state)

☐ Articles of Incorporation (filed with state)

☐ Amendments to Articles of Incorporation (filed with state)

☐ Certificate of Good Standing (requested from state)

☐ By-Laws of the corporation (in corporate record book)

☐ Amendments to the By-Laws of the corporation (in corporate record book)

☐ Minutes of first meeting of the board of directors (in corporate record book)

☐ Minutes of the first meeting of the shareholders (in corporate record book)

☐ Minutes of annual board of directors meetings (in corporate record book)

☐ Minutes of the annual meetings of the shareholders (in corporate record book)

☐ Minutes of any special board of directors meetings (in corporate record book)

☐ Minutes of any special shareholders meetings (in corporate record book)

- ☐ Shareholder proxies (in corporate record book)

- ☐ Shareholder voting agreements (in corporate record book)

- ☐ Resolutions of the board of directors (in corporate record book)

- ☐ Resolutions of the shareholders (in corporate record book)

- ☐ Corporate loans to officers or directors (in corporate record book)

- ☐ Corporate pension or profit-sharing plans (in corporate record book)

- ☐ Corporate insurance or health benefit plans (in corporate record book)

- ☐ Form and content of stock certificates (in corporate record book)

- ☐ Stock transfer book (in corporate record book)

- ☐ Corporate accounting books

- ☐ Annual financial reports (in corporate record book)

- ☐ Annual reports (filed with the state)

- ☐ Articles of Merger (filed with the state)

- ☐ Articles of Dissolution (filed with the state)

- ☐ Corporate tax records (filed with state and federal tax authorities)

- ☐ Applications to qualify as foreign corporation (filed with other states in which the corporation desires to conduct active business)

Chapter 4

Pre-Incorporation Activities

The planning stage of incorporation is vital to the success of any corporation. The structure of a new corporation, including the number of directors, number of shares of stock, and other matters, must be carefully tailored to the specific needs of the business. Attorneys typically use a pre-incorporation worksheet to assemble all of the necessary information from which to plan the incorporation process.

By filling out a pre-incorporation worksheet, potential business owners will be able to have before them all of the basic data to use in preparing the necessary incorporation paperwork. The process of preparing this worksheet will also help uncover any potential differences of opinion among the persons who are desiring to form the corporation. Often conflicts and demands are not known until the actual process of determining the corporate structure begins. Frank discussions regarding the questions of voting rights, number of directors, and other management decisions often will enable potential associates to resolve many of the difficult problems of corporate management in advance. The use of a written worksheet will also provide all persons involved with a clear and permanent record of the information. This may provide the principals of the corporation with vital support for later decisions that may be required.

All persons involved in the planned corporation should participate in the preparation of the following worksheet. Please take the time to carefully and completely fill in all of the spaces. Following the worksheet, there is a pre-incorporation checklist which provides a clear listing of all of the required actions necessary to incorporate a business. Follow this checklist carefully as the incorporation process proceeds. After this pre-incorporation checklist, there is a document filing checklist which provides a listing of the corporate documents which are normally required to be filed with the state corporation office. Finally, there is a discussion and form for reserving the corporate name with the state corporation department. If required, this will be the first form filed with the state corporation department.

Unfamiliar terms relating to corporations are explained in the glossary of this book. As the pre-incorporation worksheet is filled in, please refer to the following explanations:

Address of state corporation department: The Appendix of this book provides this address. You should write to this department immediately, requesting all available information on incorporation of a for-profit business corporation in your state. Although the forms in this book are designed for use in all states and the Appendix provides up-to-date information on state requirements, state laws and fees charged for incorporation are subject to change. Having the latest available information will save you time and trouble.

Corporate name: The selection of a corporate name is often crucial to the success of a corporation. The name must not conflict with any existing company names, nor must it be deceptively similar to other names. It is often wise to clearly explain the business of the corporation through the choice of name. All states allow for a reservation of the corporate name in advance of actual incorporation. Check the Appendix listing for your state.

Parties involved: This listing should provide the names, addresses, and phone numbers of all of the people who are involved in the planning stages of the corporation.

Principal place of business: This must be the address of the actual physical location of the main business. It may not be a post office box. If the corporation is home-based, this address should be the home address.

Purpose of corporation: Many states allow the use of an "all-purpose" business purpose clause in describing the main activity of the business; for example—to conduct any lawful business. The Articles of Incorporation which are used in this book provide this type of form. However, a few states require a specific business purpose to be identified in the Articles of Incorporation. Please check in the Appendix to see if this is a requirement in your state. If you must specify a purpose, be concise and specific but broad enough to allow for flexibility in operating your business.

State/local licenses required: Here you should note any specific requirements for licenses to operate your type of business. Most states require obtaining a tax ID number and a retail, wholesale, or sales tax license. A federal tax ID number must be obtained by all corporations. Additionally, certain types of businesses will require health department approvals, state board licensing, or other forms of licenses. If necessary, check with a competent local attorney for details regarding the types of licenses required for your locality and business type.

Patents/copyrights/trademarks: If patents, copyrights or trademarks will need to be transferred into the corporation, they should be noted here.

State of incorporation: In general, the corporation should be incorporated in the state in which it will conduct business. In the past, the state of Delaware was regarded as the best state in which to incorporate. This was due to the fact that Delaware was the first state to modernize its corporation laws to reflect the realities of present-day corporate business. This is no longer the case. Virtually all states have now enacted corporate laws very similar to those in Delaware. In the vast majority of situations, it is preferable to be incorporated in your home state.

Corporate existence: The choices here are perpetual (forever) or limited to a certain length. In virtually all cases, you should choose perpetual.

Proposed date to begin corporate business: This should be the date on which you expect the corporation to begin its legal existence. Until this date (actually, until the state formally accepts the Articles of Incorporation), the incorporators of your corporation will continue to be legally liable for any business conducted on behalf of the proposed corporation.

Incorporators: This should be the person (or persons) who will prepare and file the Articles of Incorporation. Most states allow for one incorporator. However, a few require more than one. Please check the Appendix for the requirements in your particular state.

Date of first directors meeting: This will be the date proposed for holding the first meeting of the board of directors, at which the corporate By-Laws will be officially adopted.

Proposed bank for corporate bank account: In advance of incorporation, you should determine the bank which will handle the corporate accounts. Obtain from the bank the necessary bank resolution, which will be signed by the board of directors at the first directors meeting.

Cost of incorporation: The state fees for incorporation are listed in the Appendix. This cost should also reflect the cost of obtaining professional assistance (legal or accounting); the cost of procuring the necessary supplies; and any other direct costs of the incorporation process.

Number of directors: Most states allow a corporation to have a single director. A number of states require three directors unless there are fewer than three shareholders, in which case they allow for the number of directors to equal the number of shareholders. Please check the Appendix for the requirements in your particular state.

Proposed directors: Here you should list the names and addresses of the proposed members of the first board of directors. Although not a requirement in every state, the Articles of Incorporation used in this book provides that these persons be listed. It is not possible to keep the names of the directors of a corporation secret.

Corporation's registered agent and address: Here you should list the name and actual street address of the person who will act as the registered agent of the corporation. All states (except New York) require that a specific person be available as the agent of the corporation for the service of process (that is: to accept subpoenas or summons on behalf of the corporation). The person need not be a shareholder, director, or officer of the corporation. The registered agent need not be a lawyer. Normally, the main owner, chairperson of the board of directors, or president of the corporation is selected as the registered agent.

Proposed officers: This information is not provided in the Articles of Incorporation and need not be made public. You should list here the persons who are proposed as the first officers of the business.

Out-of-state qualification: If the corporation desires to actively conduct business in a state other that the main state of incorporation, it is necessary to "qualify" the corporation in that state. This generally requires obtaining a Certificate of Authority to Transact Business from the other state. In this context, a corporation from another state is referred to as a "foreign" corporation. If you desire that your corporation qualify for activities in another state, you are advised to consult a competent business attorney.

Required quorum for shareholder's meeting: This is the percentage of ownership of shares of issued stock in the corporation which must be represented at a shareholders meeting in order to officially transact any shareholder business. This is normally set at a "majority" (over 50%), although this figure can be set higher.

Annual shareholders meeting: The date, time, and place of the annual shareholders meeting should be specified.

Required vote for shareholder action: Once it is determined that a quorum of shareholders is present at a meeting, this is the percentage of ownership of shares of issued stock in the corporation which must vote in the affirmative in order to officially pass any shareholder business. This is normally set at a "majority" (over 50%), although this figure can be set higher and can be made to be unanimous.

Fiscal year and accounting type: For accounting purposes, the fiscal year and accounting type (cash or accrual) of the corporation should be chosen in advance. Please consult with a competent accounting professional.

Amendments to Articles of Incorporation: Here should be the determination of which bodies of the corporation will have the authority to amend the Articles of Incorporation. The forms in this book are designed to allow the Articles of the corporation to be amended by the board of directors only upon approval by the shareholders.

Amendments to By-Laws: Here should be the determination of which bodies of the corporation will have the authority to amend the By-Laws. The forms in this book are designed to allow the By-Laws of the corporation to be amended by the board of directors only upon approval by the shareholders.

Annual directors meeting: The date, time, and place of the annual board of directors meeting should be specified.

Required quorum for director's meeting: This is the percentage of directors which must be present at a board of directors meeting in order to officially transact any directors business. This is normally set at a "majority" (over 50%), although this figure can be set higher.

Required vote for director action: Once it is determined that a quorum of directors is present at a meeting, this is the percentage of directors which must vote in the affirmative in order to officially pass any board of director's business. This is normally set at a "majority" (over 50%), although this figure can be set higher and can be made to be unanimous.

Initial investment: This figure is the total amount of money or property which will be transferred to the corporation upon its beginning business. This transfer will be in exchange for the issuance of shares of stock in the corporation. This is also referred to as "paid-in capital". A few states require a minimum amount of "paid-in-capital" before beginning corporate business. Please check your state's listing in the Appendix.

Initial indebtedness: If there is to be any initial indebtedness for the corporation, please list here.

Initial authorized number of shares: This figure is required to be listed in the Articles of Incorporation. The number of shares of stock to be authorized should be listed. For small corporations, this number may be influenced by the incorporation fee structure of the state of incorporation. For example, some states allow for a minimum incorporation fee when only a certain minimum number of stock shares are authorized. Please see the Appendix for the requirements in your state and check with your state corporation department.

Par value or no par value? This refers to an arbitrary indication as to the value of the stock. The designation of stock as having a certain "par" value is *not* an indication of the actual value of the shares of stock. Shares must be sold for a price at or below par value. If no par value is assigned, the shares are issued for the actual price paid per share. The choice of par or no par value stock may affect the issuance of dividends and should be referred to the corporate accountant.

Proposed sales of shares of stock: Here should be listed the names, cash or property, and value of potential sales of shares of stock which may be approved by the board of directors once the corporation is officially authorized to issue stock.

Following the Pre-Incorporation Worksheet is a Pre-Incorporation Checklist and a Document Filing Checklist. Please use these checklists to be certain that you have completed all of the necessary steps for incorporation. Once all of the persons involved have completed the Pre-Incorporation Worksheet, agreed on all of the details, and reviewed the Pre-Incorporation and Document Filing Checklists, the actual process of incorporation may begin. If the choice for a corporate name may be similar to another business or if the incorporators wish to insure that the name will be available, an Application for Reservation of Corporate Name may be filed. This is a simple form which requests that the state corporation department hold a chosen corporate name until the actual Articles of Incorporation are filed, at which time the name will become the official registered name of the corporation. Page 45 contains a sample of this form. There will be a fee required for the filing of this form and some states prefer that pre-printed state forms be used. Please check in the Appendix and with the specific state corporation department for information. In any event, the information required will be the same as is necessary for this sample form.

Pre-Incorporation Worksheet

Name/address of State Corporation Department (from Appendix)

_____

_____

_____

Proposed Name of the Corporation:

First choice _____

Alternate choices: _____

_____

Parties Involved in Forming the Corporation

Name	Address	Phone
_____	_____	_____
_____	_____	_____
_____	_____	_____
_____	_____	_____
_____	_____	_____
_____	_____	_____

Location of Business:

Address of principal place of business: _____

_____

Description of principal place of business: _____

_____

_____

Ownership of principal place of business: (Own/lease ?) _____

Other places of business: _____

_____

_____

_____

Type of Business

Purpose of corporation: _____
_____

State/local licenses required: _____
_____

Patents/copyrights/trademark: _____

Incorporation Matters

State of incorporation: _____

Corporate existence (limited or perpetual?): _____

Proposed date to begin corporate business: _____

Names and addresses of those who will act as incorporators:
    Name   Address

_____   _____
_____   _____
_____   _____

Proposed date of first directors meeting: _____

Proposed bank for corporate bank account: _____

Cost of incorporation: _____

Corporate Management

Proposed number of directors: _____

Proposed first board of directors:
    Name   Address

_____   _____
_____   _____
_____   _____

Corporation's registered agent and office address? _____
_____

Proposed first officers:

            Name   Address

President: _____ _____

Vice President: _____ _____

Secretary: _____ _____

Treasurer: _____ _____

Is qualification in other states necessary?: _____

Corporate By-Laws

Required quorum for shareholders meetings: _____

Annual Shareholders Meeting
      Place   Date   Time

_____ _____ _____

Required vote for shareholders actions: (majority/%/unanimous?): _____

Fiscal year: _____

Accounting type: (cash or accrual?): _____

Amendments to Articles: _____ directors; _____ shareholders; ____ either

Amendments to By-Laws: _____ directors; _____ shareholders; ____ either

Annual Directors Meeting
      Place   Date   Time

_____ _____ _____

Required quorum for directors meetings: _____

Required vote for directors actions: (majority/%/unanimous?): _____

Corporate Stock:

Initial investment total: $_____

Initial indebtedness: $_____

Initial authorized number of shares: _____

Par value or no par value? _____

Proposed sales of shares of stock:

Name	Cash/Property	Amount
_____	_____	_____
_____	_____	_____
_____	_____	_____
_____	_____	_____
_____	_____	_____
_____	_____	_____
_____	_____	_____

Pre-Incorporation Checklist

❑ Write state corporation office for information (see Appendix).

❑ Complete pre-incorporation checklist.

❑ Check annual fees and filing requirements.

❑ Prepare Articles of Incorporation.

❑ If desired, have attorney review Articles prior to filing.

❑ Review tax impact of incorporation with accountant.

❑ Check state tax, employment, licensing, unemployment, and worker's compensation requirements.

❑ Check insurance requirements.

❑ Procure corporate seal.

❑ Prepare stock certificates.

❑ Prepare corporate accounting ledgers.

❑ Prepare corporate record book (looseleaf binder).

Document Filing Checklist

❏ Application for Reservation of Corporate Name (if desired)

❏ Articles of Incorporation (mandatory)

❏ Amendments to Articles of Incorporation (mandatory, if applicable)

❏ Annual Corporate Reports (mandatory)

❏ Change of Address or Registered Agent (mandatory)

❏ Articles of Merger (mandatory, if applicable)

❏ Articles of Dissolution (mandatory, if applicable)

❏ Any other required state forms (see Appendix)

Application for Reservation of Corporate Name

TO:

I , _____ , with office located at
_____ ,
acting as an incorporator, apply for reservation of the following corporate name:

_____

This corporate name is intended to be used to incorporate a for-profit corporation in the State of _____ , County of
_____ .

I request that this corporate name be reserved for a period of _____ days. Please issue a certificate of reservation of this corporate name.

Dated _____ , 19 ___

_____
Signature of Incorporator

Chapter 5

Articles of Incorporation

The central legal document for any corporation is the Articles of Incorporation. In some states, this document may be called a Certificate of Incorporation, Articles of Association, or Articles of Organization. Please check the Appendix for the requirements in your particular state. This form outlines the basic structure of the corporation and details those matters which are relevant to the public registration of the corporation. The name, purpose, owners, registered agent, address, and other vital facts relating to the existence of the corporation are filed with the state by using this form. Upon filing of the Articles of Incorporation, payment of the proper fee, and acceptance by the state corporation department, the corporation officially begins its legal existence. Until the state has accepted the Articles, the incorporators are not shielded from liability by the corporate form. Some states have chosen to confuse matters slightly by referring to another form which may be issued by the state as a Certificate of Incorporation. Please check the Appendix for the state requirements for the state of your potential incorporation. For clarity, however, this book will refer to the incorporator-prepared document as the Articles of Incorporation.

There are a number of items which are required to be noted in all Articles of Incorporation. The Articles may also include many other details of the corporation's existence. Please check the Appendix and with your state incorporation department for specific details. Following is a Checklist of items which are mandatory or optional for Articles of Incorporation.

Articles of Incorporation Checklist

The mandatory details for Articles of Incorporation under most state laws are:

❒ The name of the corporation

❒ The purpose of the corporation

❒ The duration of the corporation

❒ The name and address of each incorporator

❒ The name of the registered agent of the corporation

❒ The office of the registered agent of the corporation

❒ The number of shares of stock that the corporation is authorized to issue to shareholders

❒ Amount of initial capital of corporation (optional in some states)

❒ The number, names, and addresses of the first board of directors

❒ Par value or no par value for shares of stock

❒ The signature of the incorporators

❒ The signature of the registered agent

In addition, the following items may also be included at your option:

❒ The terms and qualifications for board members

❒ Provisions relating to the powers of the directors, officers, or shareholders

❒ Designation of different classes of stock

☐ Voting and other rights or restrictions on stock

☐ Preemptive or cumulative voting rights

☐ Election to be a close corporation under state law

☐ Provisions indemnifying corporate officers and directors

The Articles of Incorporation for your corporation should include all of the required information. Since Articles are a public record, all of the information in them will be available for inspection. However, since the names of the directors will usually be required to be revealed in the annual reports that are filed with the state, there is no purpose in attempting to conceal identities of actual management of the corporation. Much of the information which is not required in the Articles may instead be put into the By-Laws of the corporation. In this manner, the actual management structure and details will remain unavailable for public inspection. Some states provide pre-printed Articles of Incorporation which are required to be used for filing. The information required, however, will be the same as is noted in the sample Articles of Incorporation in this chapter. Even if state-supplied forms are used, it will be helpful to read through this chapter and fill in the information as noted on the sample forms. Transferring it to the state form will then be a simple task.

Articles of Incorporation may be amended at any time. However, this generally requires a formal filing with the state and the issuance of a Certificate of Amendment of Articles of Incorporation. It also normally requires the payment of a fee. For these reasons, it is often a good idea to only put those items in the original Articles which are unlikely to require changes in the near future. All of the necessary information and forms for amending the Articles of Incorporation are provided in Chapter 7.

This chapter contains sample clauses for preparing Articles of Incorporation. The sample clauses in this chapter are labeled as either mandatory or optional. An explanation is also provided for each clause. You should check the Appendix and any information which you have received from the state corporation department to be certain that you have included all of the necessary information for your state. A few states may require additional Articles. Most of the information required for preparing the clauses for this form will be on your Pre-Incorporation Worksheet, which you prepared in Chapter 4. Once you have chosen which of the clauses you will use, re-type the Articles of Incorporation. (Type in the correct title for this document if your state has a different name for it—check the Appendix). They should be typed in black ink on one side of 8.5" X 11" white paper, double-spaced. If state-supplied documents are used, fill them in with the information you have prepared in this book. Optional clauses may be added to state-supplied forms where necessary.

The Articles must then be properly signed. Although not required by all states, the form in this book is designed to be notarized. A few states require that the Articles be published as legal notices in newspapers. Please check the Appendix for the requirements in your particular state. The signed Articles of Incorporation and the proper fee should be sent to the proper state office. Upon receipt, the state corporation department will check for duplication or confusing conflicts with the names of any other registered corporation. They will also check to be certain that all of the statutory requirements have been fulfilled and that the proper fee has been paid. If there is a problem, the Articles will be returned with an explanation of the difficulty. Correct the problem and re-file the Articles. If everything is in order, the business will officially be incorporated and able to begin to conduct business as a corporate entity. Some states have different procedures for indicating the beginning existence of a corporation. For example, you may need to request an official Certificate of Filing, Certificate of Good Standing, or other type of Certificate and pay a fee for this record. Check with your state corporation department. A completed sample Articles of Incorporation is included at the end of this chapter.

Title and Introduction (MANDATORY)

Check in the Appendix and with your state corporation department for any changes to this clause. If your state has a different title for this document, please insert the proper title (for example: Certificate of Incorporation of _____). The name of the corporation should include the corporate designation (see below under Name of Corporation).

Articles of Incorporation of

_____

The undersigned person(s), acting as incorporator(s) for the purpose of forming a stock business corporation under the laws of the State of _____ , adopts the following Articles of Incorporation:

Name of Corporation (MANDATORY)

The name of the corporation should be unique. It should not be confusingly similar to any other business name in use within your state. In addition, it should not contain any terms which might lead people to believe that it is a government or financial institution. Finally, it must generally contain an indication that the business is a corporation, such as Inc., Incorporated, Corporation, or Limited. Some states allow the use of the word Company in the name of corporations. Others do not. If you wish to use a term of corporate designation other than Corporation or Incorporated (or abbreviations of these), please check the Appendix and with your state corporation department.

Article 1. The name of the corporation is _____.

Purpose and Powers of the Corporation (MANDATORY)

Many states allows a general statement of purpose: "to transact any and all lawful business for which corporations may be incorporated under the Business Corporation Act of the State of _____". Others may require that you specifically state the purpose of your corporation, such as: "to operate a retail dry-cleaning business". Please check the Appendix for the requirements in your particular state. If you are required to state a specific purpose, try to be broad enough to allow your business flexibility without the necessity of later amending the Articles of Incorporation to reflect a change in direction of your business. Chose the clause appropriate for your state and circumstances. (Please note that Kentucky and Massachusetts are referred to as "Commonwealths", rather than "States".)

Article 2. The purpose for which this corporation is organized is to transact any and all lawful business for which corporations may be organized under the laws of the State of _____ , and to have all powers which are afforded corporations under the laws of the State of _____ .

Or:

> **Article 2**. The purpose for which this corporation is organized
> is:_____
> _____. This corporation shall have all powers under the
> laws of the State of _____ .

Duration of Corporation (MANDATORY)

All states allow for a perpetual duration for corporations, meaning that the corporation can continue in existence forever. Unless there is a specific business reason to indicate otherwise, this is generally the safest choice. A limited duration statement is not an acceptable method to dissolve a corporation. Please see Chapter 15 regarding corporate dissolutions.

> **Article 3**. The duration of this corporation shall be perpetual.

Minimum Capitalization (usually MANDATORY)

This clause refers to the amount of capital which will form the initial basis for operating the corporation. Several states have specific dollar amounts of minimum capital which is required for a corporation to be incorporated, ranging from $500 to $1,000. All other states have no minimum and you may delete this clause. Please check the Appendix and check with your state corporation department.

> **Article 4**. The total amount of initial capitalization of this corporation is
> $ _____ .

Authorization to Issue Stock (MANDATORY)

The number of shares of stock which will be issued is a business determination. There is no specific reason that the number of shares should be large. In fact, in some states the amount of fees charged for incorporation is based upon the number of shares which are authorized to be issued. Please check the Appendix for the requirements in your particular state.

> **Article 5**. The total number of shares of common capital stock that this corporation is authorized to issue is _____ .

Par or No Par Value (MANDATORY; may be optional)

This refers to the arbitrary value which has been assigned to your shares of stock. It does not refer to the actual purchase price required for the shares of stock. Please consult with the corporation's accountant if you have questions regarding this item. Choose the clause for Article 6 which is appropriate for your state and circumstances.

> **Article 6**. This stock shall have a par value of _____ .

Or:

> **Article 6**. This stock shall have no par value.

Name of Registered Agent (MANDATORY)

The registered agent for a corporation is the person upon whom service of process (summons, subpoena, etc.) can be served. This person must be an adult who is a resident of the state of incorporation. The usual choice is the main owner of the corporation. Residents of New York State are required to have the Secretary of State be the authorized agent for service of process. Please see the Appendix and check with your state corporation department. There is a place at the end of the Articles of Incorporation for the registered agent to sign.

> **Article 7**. The initial registered agent of this corporation is _____ . By his/her signature at the end of this document, this person acknowledges acceptance of the responsibilities as registered agent of this corporation.

Address of Registered Agent (MANDATORY)

This address must be an actual place, generally the offices of the corporation. It may not be a post office box or other unmanned location.

Article 8. The initial address of the office of the registered agent of this corporation is _____ ,
in the County of _____ , State of _____ .

Name, Address, Age of Incorporator(s) (MANDATORY)

This is the name and address of the person or persons who are filing for incorporation. The minimum age requirement for incorporating a business is generally 18. A few states allow corporations or partnerships to act as incorporators. Please check the Appendix or with your state corporation department.

Article 9. The name(s), addresses and ages of the incorporator(s) of this corporation is/are:

Name	Address	Age
_____	_____	_____
_____	_____	_____
_____	_____	_____

Number of Directors (usually MANDATORY)

The minimum number of directors allowed is generally one. However, a few states require three directors if there are over two shareholders. Thus, in those states, if there is only one shareholder, then there may be one director. If there are two shareholders, there must be two directors. But if there are three shareholders or more, there must be three directors. Please check the Appendix.

Article 10. The number of directors of this corporation is _____ .

Name and Addresses of Initial Directors (MANDATORY)

This clause provides for the initial directors of the corporation until the first meeting of the shareholders of the corporation either elect or replace these directors.

Article 11. The names and addresses of the initial directors of this corporation are as follows:

Name   Address

_____   _____

_____   _____

_____   _____

Preemptive Rights (Optional)

Using this clause, you may include any preemptive stock rights in the Articles, if desired. Preemptive rights are like a right of first refusal. If a corporation proposes to authorize new shares of stock, preemptive rights allow current shareholders the right to acquire a pro-rata percentage of the new shares based on their current percentage of ownership. This prevents their ownership percentage from being watered down by the authorization and issuance of new shares of stock. Under the laws of some states, preemptive rights exist unless the Articles of Incorporation specifically state that they do not. In other states, preemptive rights *do not* exist unless the Articles of Incorporation specifically state that they do. The best method of dealing with this issue is to include one of the following clauses which fits your circumstances.

Article 12. This corporation shall have preemptive rights for all shareholders.

Or:

Article 12. This corporation shall have no preemptive rights for any shareholders.

Preferences and Limitations on Stock (Optional)

In this clause, any voting preferences or limitations on transfers or other rights or restrictions on stock can be listed. This information may instead be listed in the By-Laws of the corporation, if preferred.

Article 13. The following are preferences and limitations on the common stock of this corporation:

_____
_____
_____ .

Additional Articles (Optional)

This clause may be used to adopt any additional articles which may be desired.

Article 14. This corporation adopts the following additional articles:

_____
_____
_____
_____ .

Closing and Signatures (MANDATORY)

This clause provides a statement certifying that the facts as stated are true and correct. It also provides for the registered agent to sign acknowledging his acceptance of the responsibilities of this job. This should be signed in front of a Notary Public.

I certify that all of the facts stated in these Articles of Incorporation are true and correct and are made for the purpose of forming a business corporation under the laws of the State of _____ .

Dated _____

_____
Signature of Incorporator

_____
Signature of Incorporator

_____
Signature of Incorporator

I acknowledge my appointment as registered agent of this corporation and accept the appointment.

Dated _____

_____
Signature of Registered Agent

State of _____   )
)   S.S.
County of _____   )

Before me, on _____ , 19 ___, personally appeared

_____
_____
and_____,
who are known to me to be the persons who subscribed their names to this document, and acknowledged that they did so for the purposes stated.

_____
Notary Public, in and for the County of _____ , State of _____. My commission expires _____, 19 ___.

Sample Completed Articles of Incorporation

Articles of Incorporation of ABCXYZ Corporation

The undersigned person, acting as incorporator for the purpose of forming a stock business corporation under the laws of the State of Superior, adopts the following Articles of Incorporation:

Article 1. The name of the corporation is ABCXYZ Corporation.

Article 2. The purpose for which this corporation is organized is to transact any and all lawful business for which corporations may be organized under the laws of the State of Superior, and to have all powers which are afforded to corporations under the laws of the state of Superior.

Article 3. The duration of this corporation shall be perpetual.

Article 4. The total amount of initial capitalization of this corporation is $ 1,000.

Article 5. The total number of shares of common capital stock that this corporation is authorized to issue is 100.

Article 6. This stock shall have no par value.

Article 7. The initial registered agent of this corporation is Mary Celeste.

Article 8. The initial address of the office of the registered agent of this corporation is 1234 Main Street, in the County of Inferior, State of Superior.

Article 9. The name, address, and age of the incorporator of this corporation is Mary Celeste, 1234 Main Street, County of Inferior, State of Superior, age 25 years.

Article 10. The number of directors of this corporation is 2 (two).

Article 11. The names and addresses of the initial directors of this corporation are as follows:

Name	Address
Mary Celeste	1234 Main Street, Capitol City, Superior
John Celeste	1234 Main Street, Capitol City, Superior

Article 12. This corporation shall have preemptive rights for all shareholders.

Article 13. The following are preferences and limitations on the common stock of this corporation: none.

Article 14. This corporation adopts the following additional articles: none.

I certify that all of the facts stated in these Articles of Incorporation are true and correct and are made for the purpose of forming a business corporation under the laws of the State of Superior.

Dated June 4, 1995

Mary Celeste
Signature of Incorporator

I acknowledge my appointment as registered agent of this corporation and accept the appointment.

Dated June 4, 1995

Mary Celeste
Signature of Registered Agent

State of Superior)
) S.S.
County of Inferior)

Before me, on June 4, 1995, personally appeared Mary Celeste, who is known to me to be the person who subscribed his/her name to this document, and acknowledged that he/she did so for the purposes stated.

Andrea Doria
Notary Public, in and for the County of Inferior, State of Superior. My commission expires June 5, 1996.

Chapter 6

Corporate By-Laws

The By-Laws of a corporation are the third part of the triangle that provides the framework for the management of the corporate business. Along with state law and the Articles of Incorporation, the By-Laws provide a clear outline of the rights and responsibilities of all parties to a corporation. In particular, the By-Laws provide the actual details of the operational framework for the business. The By-Laws are the internal document that will contain the basic rules on how the corporation is to be run. Every corporation must have a set of By-Laws. Many of the provisions cover relatively standard procedural questions, relating to quorums, voting, and stock. Other provisions may need to be specifically tailored to the type of business for which the By-Laws are intended. They are generally able to be amended by vote of the board of directors, unless the Articles of Incorporation or the By-Laws themselves have transferred that authority to the shareholders. The By-Laws provided in this book specify that the power to amend the By-Laws is vested in the board of directors, but that the shareholders have the power to approve or reject any amendment. For more information regarding the amendment of By-Laws, refer to Chapter 7.

The By-Laws can contain very specific or very general provisions for the internal management of the company. Typically, the By-Laws cover 5 general areas:

- The rights and responsibilities of the shareholders
- The rights and responsibilities of the directors

- The rights and responsibilities of the officers
- Financial matters
- Methods for amending the By-Laws

This chapter contains sample clauses for preparing your corporate By-Laws. Once you have chosen which of the clauses you will use and have filled in any required information, re-type the By-Laws in black ink on one side of 8.5" X 11" white paper, double-spaced. A completed sample set of By-Laws is included at the end of this chapter. Your completed By-Laws should be both formally adopted at the first board of directors meeting and approved at the first shareholders meeting. The following is a Checklist for use in preparing your By-Laws:

By-Laws Checklist

❒ Power to designate the location of principal office of corporation

❒ Power to designate the registered office and agent of corporation

❒ Date, time, and place of annual shareholders meeting

❒ Procedures for special shareholders meetings

❒ Notice and waivers for shareholders meetings

❒ Voting eligibility requirements for shareholders

❒ Quorum and votes required for actions for shareholders

❒ Shareholders proxy requirements

❒ Shareholder consent resolutions

❒ Cumulative voting requirements

❒ Powers of the directors

❒ How many directors?

❒ Term of office for directors

❐ Directors election procedures

❐ Date, time and, place of annual directors meeting

❐ Procedures for special directors meetings

❐ Notice and waivers for directors meetings

❐ Quorum and votes required for actions for directors

❐ Directors consent resolutions

❐ Removing and filling vacancies of directors

❐ Salaries of directors

❐ Fiduciary duties of directors

❐ How many officers and how long the term of office?

❐ Removing and filling vacancies of officers

❐ Salaries of officers

❐ Duties of the officers

❐ How are stock certificates handled?

❐ Are there any restrictions on the rights to transfer shares of stock?

❐ How are corporate financial matters to be handled?

❐ Can officers or directors borrow money from the corporation?

❐ By-Law amendment procedures

Title

By-Laws of _____ ,
   a corporation incorporated under the laws of the
         State of _____ .

Corporate Office and Registered Agent

1. Corporate Office and Registered Agent. The board of directors has the power to determine the location of the corporation's principal place of business and registered office, which need not be the same location. The board of directors also has the power to designate the corporation's registered agent, who may be an officer or director.

Date and Time of Shareholders Annual Meeting

2. Date and Time of Shareholders Annual Meeting. The annual shareholders meeting will be held on the _____ of every year at _____ m. This meeting is for the purpose of electing directors and for transacting any other necessary business. If this day is a legal holiday, the meeting will be held on the next day.

Shareholders Special Meetings

3. **Shareholders Special Meetings**. Special meetings of the shareholders may be called at any time and for any purpose. These meetings may be called by either the president or the board of directors or upon request of _____ percent of the shareholders of the corporation. The request for a special meeting must be made in writing which states the time, place, and purpose of the meeting. The request should be given to the secretary of the corporation who will prepare and send written notice to all shareholders of record who are entitled to vote at the meeting.

Place of Shareholders Meetings

4. **Place of Shareholders Meetings**. The board of directors has the power to designate the place for shareholders meetings, unless a waiver of notice of the meeting signed by all shareholders designates the place for the meeting. If no place is designated, either by the board of directors or all of the shareholders, then the place for the meeting will be the principal office of the corporation.

Notice of Shareholders Meetings

5. **Notice of Shareholders Meetings**. Written notice of shareholders meetings must be sent to each shareholder of record entitled to vote at the meeting. The notice must be sent no less than _____ days nor more than _____ days before the date of the meeting. The notice should be sent to the shareholder's address as shown in the corporate Stock Transfer Book. The notice will include the place, date, and time of the meeting. Notices for special meetings must also include the purpose of the meeting. When notices are sent, the secretary of the corporation must prepare an Affidavit of Mailing of Notices. Shareholders may waive notice of meetings if done in writing, except that attendance at a meeting is considered a waiver of notice of the meeting.

Shareholders Entitled to Notice, to Vote, or to Dividends

6. Shareholders Entitled to Notice, to Vote, or to Dividends. For the purpose of determining which shareholders are entitled to notice, to vote at meetings, or to receive dividends, the board of directors may order that the corporate Stock Transfer Books be closed for _____ days prior to a meeting or the issuance of a dividend. The shareholders entitled to receive notice, vote at meetings, or receive dividends are those who are recorded in the Stock Transfer Book upon the closing of the Book. Instead of closing the Books, the board of directors may also set a Record Date. The shareholders recorded in the Stock Transfer Book at the close of business on the Record Date will be entitled to receive notice, vote at meetings, or receive dividends. A list of shareholders entitled to receive notice, vote at meetings, or receive dividends will be prepared by the secretary when necessary and provided to the officers of the corporation. Every shareholder who is entitled to receive notice, vote, or receive dividends is also entitled to examine this list and the corporate stock transfer book.

Shareholders Quorum

7. Shareholders Quorum. A quorum for shareholders meeting will be a majority of the outstanding shares which are entitled to vote at the meeting, whether in person or represented by proxy. Once a quorum is present, business may be conducted at the meeting, even if shareholders leave prior to adjournment.

Shareholders Proxies

8. Shareholders Proxies. At all meetings of shareholders, a shareholder may vote by signed proxy or by power of attorney. To be valid, a proxy must be filed with the secretary of the corporation prior to the stated time of the meeting. No proxy may be valid for over 11 months, unless the proxy specifically states otherwise. Proxies may always be revokable prior to the meeting for which it is intended. Attendance at the meeting for which a proxy has been authorized always revokes the proxy.

Shareholders Voting

9. Voting. Each outstanding share of the corporation which is entitled to vote as shown on the Stock Transfer Book will have one vote. The vote of the holders of a majority of the shares entitled to vote will be sufficient to decide any matter, unless a greater number is required by the Articles of Incorporation or by state law. Adjournment shall be by majority vote of those shares entitled to vote.

Shareholders Consent Resolutions

10. Shareholder Consent Resolutions. Any action which may be taken at a shareholders meeting may be taken instead without a meeting if a resolution is consented to, in writing, by all shareholders who would be entitled to vote.

Shareholders Cumulative Voting Rights

11. Shareholders Cumulative Voting rights. For the election of directors, each shareholder may vote in a cumulative manner, if desired, which will mean that if each shareholder has one vote per director to be elected, the shareholder may vote all votes for a single director or spread the votes among the directors.

Powers of the Board of Directors

12. Powers of the Board of Directors. The affairs of the corporation will be managed by the board of directors. The board of directors will have all powers available under state law, including the power to appoint and remove officers, agents, and employees; the power to change the offices, registered agent, and registered office of the corporation; the power to issue shares of stock; the power to borrow money on behalf of the corporation, including the power to execute any evidence of indebtedness on behalf of the corporation; and the power to enter into contracts on behalf of the corporation.

Number of Directors and Term of Office

13. Number of Directors and Term of Office. The number of directors will be as shown in the Articles of Incorporation and may be amended. The number is currently _____ . Each director will hold office for _____ year(s) and will be elected at the annual meeting of the shareholders.

Date and Time of Annual Meeting of the Board of Directors

14. Date and Time of Annual Meeting of the Board of Directors. The annual board of directors meeting will be held on the _____ of every year at _____ m. This meeting is for the purpose of appointing officers and for transacting any other necessary business. If this day is a legal holiday, the meeting will be held on the next day.

Special Meetings of the Board of Directors

15. Special Meetings of the Board of Directors. Special meetings of the board of directors may be called at any time and for any purpose. These meetings may be called by either the president or the board of directors. The request for a special meeting must be made in writing which states the time, place, and purpose of the meeting. The request should be given to the secretary of the corporation who will prepare and send written notice to all directors.

Place of Board of Directors Meetings

16. Place of Board of Directors Meetings. The board of directors has the power to designate the place for directors meetings. If no place is designated, then the place for the meeting will be the principal office of the corporation.

Notice of Board of Directors Meetings

17. Notice of Board of Directors Meetings. Written notice of board of directors meetings must be sent to each director. The notice must be sent no less than _____ days nor more than _____ days before the date of the meeting. The notice should be sent to the director's address as shown in the corporate records. The notice will include the place, date, and time of the meeting, and for special meetings the purpose of the meeting. When notices are sent, the secretary of the corporation must prepare an Affidavit of Mailing of Notices. directors may waive notice of meetings if done in writing, except that attendance at a meeting is considered a waiver of notice of the meeting.

Board of Directors Quorum

18. Board of Directors Quorum. A quorum for directors meetings will be a majority of the directors. Once a quorum is present, business may be conducted at the meeting, even if directors leave prior to adjournment.

Board of Directors Voting

19. Board of Directors Voting. Each director will have one vote. The vote of a majority of the directors will be sufficient to decide any matter, unless a greater number is required by the Articles of Incorporation or state law. Adjournment shall be by majority vote.

Board of Directors Consent Resolutions

20. Board of Directors Consent Resolutions. Any action which may be taken at a directors meeting may be taken instead without a meeting if a resolution is consented to, in writing, by all directors.

Removal of Directors

21. Removal of Directors. A director may be removed from office, with or without cause, at a special meeting of the shareholders called for that purpose.

Filling Directors Vacancies

22. Filling Directors Vacancies. A vacancy on the board of directors may be filled by majority vote of the remaining directors, even if technically less than a quorum. A director elected to fill a remaining term will hold office until the next annual shareholders meeting.

Salaries of Directors

23. Salaries of Directors. The salaries of the directors will be fixed by the board of directors and may be altered at any time by the board. A director may receive a salary even if she/he receives a salary as an officer.

Fiduciary Duty of Directors

24. Fiduciary Duty of Directors. Each director owes a a fiduciary duty of good faith and reasonable care with regard to all actions taken on behalf of the corporation. Each director must perform her/his duties in good faith in a manner which she/he reasonably believes to be in the best interests of the corporation, using ordinary care and prudence.

Number of Officers

25. Number of Officers. The officers of the corporation will include a president, vice-president, treasurer, and secretary. Any two or more offices may be held by the same person.

Appointment and Terms of Officers

26. Appointment and Terms of Officers. The officers of the corporation will be appointed by the directors at the first meeting of the board of directors. Each officer will hold office until death, resignation, or removal by the board of directors.

Removal of Officers

27. Removal of Officers. Any officer may be removed by the board of directors, with or without cause. Appointment of an officer does not create any contract rights for the officer.

Filling Officers Vacancies

28. Filling Officers Vacancies. A vacancy in any office for any reason may be filled by the board of directors for the unexpired term.

Duties of the President

29. Duties of the President. The president is the principal executive officer of the corporation and is subject to control by the board of directors. The president will supervise and control all of the business and activities of the corporation. The president will preside at all shareholders and directors meetings, and perform any other duties as prescribed by the board of directors.

Duties of the Vice-President

30. Duties of the Vice-President. If the president is absent, dies, or is incapacitated, the vice-president will perform the duties of the president. When acting for the president, the vice-president will have all of the powers and authority of the president. The vice-president will also perform any other duties as prescribed by the board of directors.

Duties of the Secretary

31. Duties of the Secretary. The secretary will keep the minutes of all shareholders and directors meetings. The secretary will provide notices of all meetings as required by the By-Laws. The secretary will be the custodian of the corporate records, corporate stock transfer book, and corporate seal. The secretary will keep a list of all shareholders, directors, and officers addresses. The secretary will sign, along with other officers, the corporation's stock certificates. The secretary will also perform any other duties as prescribed by the board of directors.

Duties of the Treasurer

32. Duties of the Treasurer. The treasurer will be custodian of all corporate funds and securities. The treasurer will receive and pay out funds which are receivable or payable to the corporation from any source. The treasurer will deposit all corporate funds received into the corporate bank accounts as designated by the board of directors. The treasurer will also perform any other duties as prescribed by the board of directors.

Salaries of Officers

33. Salaries of Officers. The salaries of the officers will be fixed by the board of directors and may be altered at any time by the board. An officer may receive a salary even if she/he receives a salary as a director.

Stock Certificates

34. Stock Certificates. Certificates which represent shares of ownership in the corporation will be in the form designated by the board of directors. Certificates will be signed by all officers of the corporation. Certificates will be consecutively numbered. The name and address of the person receiving the issued shares, the certificate number, the number of shares and the date of issue will be recorded by the secretary of the corporation in the corporate stock transfer book. Shares of the corporation's stock may only be transferred on the stock transfer book of the corporation by the holder of the shares in whose name they were issued as shown on the stock transfer book, or by his or her legal representative.

Financial Matters

35. Financial Matters. The board of directors will determine the accounting methods and fiscal year of the corporation. All checks, drafts, or other methods for payment shall be signed by an officer determined by resolution of the board of directors. All notes, mortgages, or other evidence of indebtedness shall be signed by an officer determined by resolution of the board of directors. No money will be borrowed or loaned by the corporation unless authorized by a resolution of the board of directors. No contracts will be entered into on behalf of the corporation unless authorized by a resolution of the board of directors. No documents may be executed on behalf of the corporation unless authorized by a resolution of the board of directors. A board of Director's resolution may be for specific instances or a general authorization.

Loans to Officers or Directors

36. Loans to Officers or Directors. The corporation may not lend any money to an officer or director of the corporation unless the loan has been approved by a majority of the shares of all stock of the corporation, including those shares that do not have voting rights.

Amendments to the By-Laws

37. Amendments to the By-Laws. These By-Laws may be amended in any manner by majority vote of the board of directors at any annual or special meeting. Any amendments by the board of directors are subject to approval by majority vote of the shareholders at any annual or special meeting.

Signatures Clause

Dated _____

_____
Secretary of the Corporation

Adopted by the board of directors on _____ , 19 ___

_____
Chairperson of the board

Approved by the Shareholders on _____ , 19 ___

_____
Secretary of the Corporation

Sample Corporate By-Laws

By-Laws of ABCXYZ Corporation, a corporation incorporated under the laws of the State of Superior.

1. **Corporate Office and Registered Agent.** The board of directors has the power to determine the location of the corporation's principal place of business and registered office, which need not be the same location. The board of directors also has the power to designate the corporation's registered agent, who may be an officer or director.

2. **Date and Time of Shareholders Annual Meeting.** The annual shareholders meeting will be held on the First Tuesday in October of every year at 10:00 a.m. This meeting is for the purpose of electing directors and for transacting any other necessary business. If this day is a legal holiday, the meeting will be held on the next day.

3. **Shareholders Special Meetings.** Special meetings of the shareholders may be called at any time and for any purpose. These meetings may be called by either the president or the board of directors or upon request of 25% percent of the shareholders of the corporation. The request for a special meeting must be made in writing which states the time, place and purpose of the meeting. The request should be given to the secretary of the corporation who will prepare and send written notice to all shareholders of record who are entitled to vote at the meeting.

4. **Place of Shareholders Meetings.** The board of directors has the power to designate the place for shareholders meetings, unless a waiver of notice of the meeting signed by all shareholders designates the place for the meeting. If no place is designated, either by the board of directors or all of the shareholders, then the place for the meeting will be the principal office of the corporation.

5. **Notice of Shareholders Meetings.** Written notice of shareholders meetings must be sent to each shareholder of record entitled to vote at the meeting. The notice must be sent no less than 7 days nor more than 21 days before the date of the meeting. The notice should be sent to the shareholder's address as shown in the corporate Stock Transfer Book. The notice will include the place, date, and time of the meeting. Notices for special meetings must

also include the purpose of the meeting. When notices are sent, the secretary of the corporation must prepare an Affidavit of Mailing of Notices. Shareholders may waive notice of meetings if done in writing, except that attendance at a meeting is considered a waiver of notice of the meeting.

6. **Shareholders Entitled to Notice, to Vote, or to Dividends.** For the purpose of determining which shareholders are entitled to notice, to vote at meetings, or to receive dividends, the board of directors may order that the corporate Stock Transfer Books be closed for 30 days prior to a meeting or the issuance of a dividend. The shareholders entitled to receive notice, vote at meetings, or receive dividends are those who are recorded in the Stock Transfer Book upon the closing of the Book. Instead of closing the Books, the board of directors may also set a Record Date. The shareholders recorded in the Stock Transfer Book at the close of business on the Record Date will be entitled to receive notice, vote at meetings, or receive dividends. A list of shareholders entitled to receive notice, vote at meetings, or receive dividends will be prepared by the secretary when necessary and provided to the officers of the corporation. Every shareholder who is entitled to receive notice, vote, or receive dividends is also entitled to examine this list and the corporate stock transfer book.

7. **Shareholders Quorum.** A quorum for shareholders meeting will be a majority of the outstanding shares which are entitled to vote at the meeting, whether in person or represented by proxy. Once a quorum is present, business may be conducted at the meeting, even if shareholders leave prior to adjournment.

8. **Shareholders Proxies.** At all meetings of shareholders, a shareholder may vote by signed proxy or by power of attorney. To be valid, a proxy must be filed with the secretary of the corporation prior to the stated time of the meeting. No proxy may be valid for over 11 months, unless the proxy specifically states otherwise. Proxies may always be revokable prior to the meeting for which it is intended. Attendance at the meeting for which a proxy has been authorized always revokes the proxy.

9. **Shareholders Voting.** Each outstanding share of the corporation which is entitled to vote as shown on the Stock Transfer Book will have one vote. The vote of the holders of a majority of the shares entitled to vote will be sufficient to decide any matter, unless a greater number is required by the Articles of Incorporation or by state law.

Adjournment shall be by majority vote of those shares entitled to vote.

10. **Shareholder Consent Resolutions.** Any action which may be taken at a shareholders meeting may be taken instead without a meeting if a resolution is consented to, in writing, by all shareholders who would be entitled to vote on the matter.

11. **Shareholders Cumulative Voting.** For the election of directors, each shareholder may vote in a Cumulative manner, if desired. Cumulative voting will mean that if each shareholder has one vote per director to be elected, the shareholder may vote all votes for a single director or spread the votes among directors in any manner.

12. **Powers of the Board of Directors.** The affairs of the corporation will be managed by the board of directors. The board of directors will have all powers available under state law, including the power to appoint and remove officers, agents, and employees; the power to change the offices, registered agent, and registered office of the corporation; the power to issue shares of stock; the power to borrow money on behalf of the corporation, including the power to execute any evidence of indebtedness on behalf of the corporation; and the power to enter into contracts on behalf of the corporation.

13. **Number of Directors and Term of Office.** The number of directors will be as shown in the Articles of Incorporation and may be amended. The number is currently three (3). Each director will hold office for one (1) year and will be elected at the annual meeting of the shareholders.

14. **Date and Time of Annual Meeting of the Board of Directors.** The annual board of directors meeting will be held on the First Tuesday of October of every year at 11:00 p.m. This meeting is for the purpose of appointing officers and for transacting any other necessary business. If this day is a legal holiday, the meeting will be held on the next day.

15. **Special Meetings of the Board of Directors.** Special meetings of the board of directors may be called at any time and for any purpose. These meetings may be called by either the president or the board of directors. The request for a special meeting must be made in writing which states the time, place and purpose of the meeting. The request should be given to the secretary of the corporation who will prepare and send written notice to all directors.

16. **Place of Board of Directors Meetings**. The board of directors has the power to designate the place for directors meetings. If no place is designated, then the place for the meeting will be the principal office of the corporation.

17. **Notice of Board of Directors Meetings**. Written notice of board of directors meetings must be sent to each director. The notice must be sent no less than 7 days nor more than 21 days before the date of the meeting. The notice should be sent to the director's address as shown in the corporate records. The notice will include the place, date, and time of the meeting, and for special meetings the purpose of the meeting. When notices are sent, the secretary of the corporation must prepare an Affidavit of Mailing of Notices. directors may waive notice of meetings if done in writing, except that attendance at a meeting is considered a waiver of notice of the meeting.

18. **Board of Directors Quorum**. A quorum for directors meetings will be a majority of the directors. Once a quorum is present, business may be conducted at the meeting, even if directors leave prior to adjournment.

19. **Board of Directors Voting**. Each director will have one vote. The vote of a majority of the directors will be sufficient to decide any matter, unless a greater number is required by the Articles of Incorporation or state law. Adjournment shall be by majority vote.

20. **Board of Directors Consent Resolutions**. Any action which may be taken at a directors meeting may be taken instead without a meeting if a resolution is consented to, in writing, by all directors.

21. **Removal of Directors**. A director may be removed from office, with or without cause, at a special meeting of the shareholders called for that purpose.

22. **Filling Directors Vacancies**. A vacancy on the board of directors may be filled by majority vote of the remaining directors, even if technically less than a quorum. A director elected to fill a remaining term will hold office until the next annual shareholders meeting.

23. **Salaries of Directors**. The salaries of the directors will be fixed by the board of directors and may be altered at any time by the board. A director may receive a salary even if she/he receives a salary as an officer.

24. **Fiduciary Duty of Directors**. Each director owes a a fiduciary duty of good faith and reasonable care with regard to all actions taken on behalf of the corporation. Each director must perform her/his duties in good faith in a manner which she/he reasonably believes to be in the best interests of the corporation, using ordinary care and prudence.

25. **Number of Officers**. The officers of the corporation will include a president, vice-president, treasurer, and secretary. Any two or more offices may be held by the same person.

26. **Appointment and Terms of Officers**. The officers of the corporation will be appointed by the directors at the first meeting of the board of directors. Each officer will hold office until death, resignation or removal by the board of directors.

27. **Removal of Officers**. Any officer may be removed by the board of directors, with or without cause. Appointment of an officer does not create any contract rights for the officer.

28. **Filling Officers Vacancies**. A vacancy in any office for any reason may be filled by the board of directors for the unexpired term.

29. **Duties of the President**. The president is the principal executive officer of the corporation and is subject to control by the board of directors. The president will supervise and control all of the business and activities of the corporation. The president will preside at all shareholders and directors meetings, and perform any other duties as prescribed by the board of directors.

30. **Duties of the Vice-President**. If the president is absent, dies, or is incapacitated, the vice-president will perform the duties of the president. When acting for the president, the vice-president will have all of the powers and authority of the president. The vice-president will also perform any other duties as prescribed by the board of directors.

31. **Duties of the Secretary**. The secretary will keep the minutes of all shareholders and directors meetings. The secretary will provide notices of all meetings as required by the By-Laws. The secretary will be the custodian of the corporate records, corporate stock transfer book, and corporate seal. The secretary will keep a list of all shareholders, directors, and officers addresses. The secretary will sign, along with other officers, the corporation's stock certificates.

The secretary will also perform any other duties as prescribed by the board of directors.

32. **Duties of the Treasurer**. The treasurer will be custodian of all corporate funds and securities. The treasurer will receive and pay out funds which are receivable or payable to the corporation from any source. The treasurer will deposit all corporate funds received into the corporate bank accounts as designated by the board of directors. The treasurer will also perform any other duties as prescribed by the board of directors.

33. **Salaries of Officers**. The salaries of the officers will be fixed by the board of directors and may be altered at any time by the board. An officer may receive a salary even if she/he receives a salary as a director.

34. **Stock Certificates**. Certificates which represent shares of ownership in the corporation will be in the form designated by the board of directors. Certificates will be signed by all officers of the corporation. Certificates will be consecutively numbered. The name and address of the person receiving the issued shares, the certificate number, the number of shares and the date of issue will be recorded by the secretary of the corporation in the corporate stock transfer book. Shares of the corporation's stock may only be transferred on the stock transfer book of the corporation by the holder of the shares in whose name they were issued as shown on the stock transfer book, or by his or her legal representative.

35. **Financial Matters**. The board of directors will determine the accounting methods and fiscal year of the corporation. All checks, drafts, or other methods for payment shall be signed by an officer determined by resolution of the board of directors. All notes, mortgages, or other evidence of indebtedness shall be signed by an officer determined by resolution of the board of directors. No money will be borrowed or loaned by the corporation unless authorized by a resolution of the board of directors. No contracts will be entered into on behalf of the corporation unless authorized by a resolution of the board of directors. No documents may be executed on behalf of the corporation unless authorized by a resolution of the board of directors. A board of Director's resolution may be for specific instances or a general authorization.

36. **Loans to Officers or Directors**. The corporation may not lend any money to an officer or director of the corporation unless the loan

has been approved by a majority of the shares of all stock of the corporation, including those shares that do not have voting rights.

37. **Amendments to the By-Laws.** These By-Laws may be amended in any manner by majority vote of the board of directors at any annual or special meeting. Any amendments by the board of directors are subject to approval by majority vote of the shareholders at any annual or special meeting.

Dated June 10, 1995

Mary Celeste
Secretary of the Corporation

Approved by the board of directors on June 14, 1995

John Celeste
Chairperson of the board

Approved by the Shareholders on June 14, 1995

Mary Celeste
Secretary of the Corporation

Chapter 7

Amendments to Corporate Articles and By-Laws

Amendments to the Articles of Incorporation and corporate By-Laws may sometimes be required by changing business circumstances. However, in general, amendments should be infrequent and reserved only for situations which require a substantial change in the manner in which the corporation conducts its business. Generally, amendments to Articles of Incorporation require that the corporation file a Certificate of Amendment or some similar form with the state. This procedure insures that the public record of the corporation's existence reflects the actual management of the corporation. The necessity of having to file any amendments to the Articles of Incorporation with the state, however, also requires that a state fee be paid. In some states, this fee can be substantial.

Under most state corporation laws, the Articles of Incorporation are amended by a process which includes both the directors of the corporation and its shareholders. The process used in this book requires that the directors approve a resolution adopting the amendment and calling for a meeting of the shareholders. At the shareholders meeting, the shareholders then approve the amendment to the Articles. Finally, a Certificate of Amendment is prepared. The final step is the filing of the Certificate with the state. The procedure used in this book for amendments to the By-Laws provides that the board of directors may amend the By-Laws, subject to approval by the shareholders, without notification of the state. (See Chapter 6). Checklists for both procedures follow.

Amendment to Articles of Incorporation Checklist

❑ A special meeting of the board of directors is called for the purpose of proposing an amendment to the Articles of Incorporation.

❑ Proper notice (or waivers) of the meeting is provided to all directors. (See Chapter 8).

❑ At the board meeting, a resolution is adopted proposing an amendment and calling for a special shareholders meeting. (A sample resolution is included in this chapter).

❑ Proper notice (or waivers) of the meeting is provided to all shareholders. (See Chapter 9).

❑ At the shareholders meeting, a resolution is adopted approving the amendment. (A sample resolution is included in this chapter).

❑ The Secretary of the corporation prepares a Certificate of Amendment of the Articles of Incorporation. (A sample Certificate is included in this chapter).

❑ The Secretary of the corporation files the Certificate with the state corporation department and pays the proper fees.

❑ The Secretary of the corporation files a copy of the Certificate in the corporate record book.

Amendment to By-Laws Checklist

❑ A special meeting of the board of directors is called for the purpose of proposing an amendment to the By-Laws.

❑ Proper notice (or waivers) of the meeting is provided to all directors. (See Chapter 7).

❑ At the board meeting, a resolution is adopted amending the By-Laws and calling for a special shareholders meeting. (A sample resolution is included in this chapter).

❑ Proper notice (or waivers) of the meeting is provided to all shareholders. (See Chapter 8).

❑ At the shareholders meeting, a resolution is adopted approving the amendment. (A sample resolution is included in this chapter).

❑ The Secretary of the corporation attaches the amendment to the original By-Laws of the corporation in the corporate record books.

Resolution of the Board of Directors of _____ Adopting Amendment to Articles of Incorporation

A meeting of the board of directors of this corporation was duly called and held on _____ , 19 ___. A quorum of the board of directors was present and at the meeting it was decided, by majority vote, that it is advisable to amend the Articles of Incorporation.

Therefore, it is
RESOLVED, that Articles of Incorporation of this corporation be amended in the following manner:

It is further
RESOLVED, that a special meeting of the shareholders of this corporation be held on _____ , 19 ___ at _____ m. at the offices of the corporation located at _____ for the purpose of obtaining shareholder approval of this amendment. The Secretary is directed to give appropriate notice to all shareholders entitled to attend this meeting. The officers of this corporation are hereby authorized to perform all necessary acts to carry out this resolution.

The undersigned, _____ , certifies that he or she is the duly elected Secretary of this corporation and that the above is a true and correct copy of the resolution that was duly adopted at a meeting of the board of directors which was held in accordance with state law and the By-Laws of the corporation on _____ , 19 ___ . I further certify that such resolution is now in full force and effect.

Dated _____

Seal

_____
Secretary of the corporation

Resolution and Consent of Shareholders of _____ Approving Amendment to Articles of Incorporation

A meeting of the shareholders of this corporation was duly called and held on _____ , 19 ___. A quorum of the shareholders was present, in person or by proxy, and at the meeting it was decided, by vote of holders of a majority of outstanding shares, that the Articles of Incorporation of this corporation be amended.

Therefore, it is
RESOLVED, that the Articles of Incorporation of this corporation be amended as follows:

Shareholders holding a majority of outstanding shares of stock in this corporation have signed this resolution and consent to this Amendment. The Secretary of this corporation is authorized to prepare and execute an official Certificate of Amendment to the Articles of Incorporation and file and record this Certificate as required. The officers of this corporation are authorized to perform all necessary acts to carry out this resolution.

Shareholder Name   Signature

_____   _____

_____   _____

_____   _____

_____   _____

_____   _____

_____   _____

_____   _____

_____   _____

The undersigned, _____ ,
certifies that he or she is the duly elected Secretary of this corporation
and that the above is a true and correct copy of the resolution that was
duly adopted at a meeting of the shareholders which was held in
accordance with state law and the By-Laws of the corporation on
_____, 19 ___ . I further certify that such resolution is
now in full force and effect.

Dated _____

                                          Seal

_____
Secretary of the corporation

Certificate of Amendment of Articles
of Incorporation of _____

Pursuant to law and the By-Laws of this corporation, a special meeting of the shareholders of this corporation was held on _____ , 19 ___ , at ____ m. at the offices of the corporation located at

_____ .

At this meeting, it was resolved by a vote of the holders of a majority of shares entitled to vote on this matter that the Articles of Incorporation of this corporation be amended to read as follows:

The undersigned, _____ , certifies that he or she is the duly elected Secretary of this corporation and that the above is a true and correct copy of the Amendment to the Articles of Incorporation that was duly adopted at a meeting of the shareholders which was held in accordance with state law and the By-Laws of the corporation on _____ , 19 ___ .

Dated _____

Seal

_____
Secretary of the corporation

Resolution of the Board of Directors of _____ Amending By-Laws and Calling for Special Meeting

A meeting of the board of directors of this corporation was duly called and held on _____ , 19 ___. A quorum of the board of directors was present and at the meeting it was decided, by majority vote, that it is advisable to amend the By-Laws of the corporation:

Therefore, it is
RESOLVED, that the By-Laws of this corporation be amended in the following manner:

It is further
RESOLVED, that a special meeting of the shareholders of this corporation be held on _____ , 19 ___ at _____ m. at the offices of the corporation located at _____
for the purpose of obtaining shareholder approval of this action. The Secretary is directed to give appropriate notice to all shareholders entitled to attend this meeting. The officers of this corporation are hereby authorized to perform all necessary acts to carry out this resolution.

The undersigned, _____ ,
certifies that he or she is the duly elected Secretary of this corporation and that the above is a true and correct copy of the resolution that was duly adopted at a meeting of the board of directors which was held in accordance with state law and the By-Laws of the corporation on _____ , 19 ___ . I further certify that such resolution is now in full force and effect.

Dated _____

Seal

_____
Secretary of the corporation

Resolution and Consent of the Shareholders of _____ Approving Amendment of the By-Laws

A meeting of the shareholders of this corporation was duly called and held on _____ , 19 ___. A quorum of the shareholders was present, in person or by proxy, and at the meeting it was decided, by vote of holders of a majority of outstanding shares, that the Amendment to the By-Laws of the corporation which was adopted at a meeting of the board of directors held on _____ , 19 ___, be approved.

Therefore, it is
RESOLVED, that the shareholders approve the amendment to the By-Laws of the corporation adopted by the board of directors of this corporation as follows:

Shareholders holding a majority of outstanding shares of stock in this corporation have signed this resolution and consent to this Amendment. The officers of this corporation are authorized to perform all necessary acts to carry out this resolution.

Shareholder Name   Signature

_____   _____

_____   _____

_____   _____

_____   _____

_____   _____

_____   _____

_____   _____

The undersigned, _____ ,
certifies that he or she is the duly elected Secretary of this corporation
and that the above is a true and correct copy of the resolution that was
duly adopted at a meeting of the Shareholders which was held in
accordance with state law and the By-Laws of the corporation on
_____ , 19 ___ . I further certify that such resolution is
now in full force and effect.

Dated _____

                                            Seal

_____
Secretary of the corporation

Chapter 8

Corporate Directors Meetings

The board of directors of a corporation transacts business as a group. Each individual director has no authority to bind the corporation (unless the board of directors as a group has previously authorized him or her to exercise that power). Even in a corporation with a single director, there must be formal records of meetings and of the resolutions adopted by the board.

Corporate boards of directors must, at a minimum, hold an annual meeting to appoint the officers of the corporation for the coming year, decide if dividends will be declared for the year, and make any other annual decisions regarding the financial matters of the business. Typically, boards will hold special meetings for specific topics much more frequently. Whenever official corporate matters are discussed as a group, the board of directors should hold a meeting, keep minutes, and record the decisions made as corporate resolutions. This is not a difficult task and it will provide a clear record of the agreements made by the board for future reference. Prior to any annual or special meetings of the board, notice must be given to each board member according to the time limits set in the By-Laws. A formal affidavit of mailing of notice should also be prepared. If all board members are in agreement, an easier method to fulfill the notice requirement is to have the board sign waivers of notice. This document and all of the other documents necessary to conduct and record board meetings are contained in this chapter. Before each type of board meeting is a Checklist of the information necessary to fill in the minutes and other forms. Follow the appropriate Checklist for each meeting.

First Directors Meeting Checklist

The following information should be covered and documented in the minutes of the first board of directors meeting:

❏ Name of corporation

❏ Date of meeting

❏ Location of meeting

❏ Officers present at meeting

❏ Others present at meeting

❏ Name of temporary Chairperson presiding over meeting

❏ Name of temporary Secretary acting at meeting

❏ Meeting called to order and quorum present

❏ Proper notification of meeting

  ❏ Notices sent and affidavit filed / or waivers filed

❏ Articles of Incorporation filed with state

  ❏ Date of filing

  ❏ Effective date of incorporation

❏ Approve and ratify any acts of incorporators taken on behalf of the corporation prior to effective date of incorporation.

❏ Elect officers of corporation.

❏ Decide on annual salaries of officers.

- ❏ Direct that any organizational expenses be reimbursed to incorporators.

- ❏ Authorize opening of corporate bank account.

- ❏ Approve corporate seal, stock certificate, and stock transfer book.

- ❏ Approve corporate By-Laws.

- ❏ Approve issuance of stock in exchange for transfers of property or money.

- ❏ Designate fiscal year dates.

- ❏ Designate accounting basis (cash or accrual basis).

- ❏ Document any other necessary business.

- ❏ Adjournment of meeting

- ❏ Date and Secretary signature on minutes

Notice of First Board of Directors
Meeting of _____

TO:

In accordance with the By-Laws of this corporation, the first organizational meeting of the board of directors will be held at _____ m., on _____ , 19 ___ , at the offices of the corporation located at

_____

_____ .

Dated _____

_____
Signature
Incorporator: _____

_____
Signature
Incorporator: _____

_____
Signature
Incorporator: _____

Affidavit of Mailing of Notice of First Board of Directors Meeting of _____

State of _____)

County of _____)

Being duly sworn, _____ states:
I am the Secretary of _____ , a
corporation organized under the laws of the State of
_____ .

On _____ , 19 ___ , I personally deposited stamped and
sealed copies of Notice of the First Directors Meeting of this corporation
in a post-office box in the City of _____ , in the State of
_____ .

The copies were correctly addressed to the following persons:

Name   Address

_____   _____

_____   _____

_____   _____

_____
Secretary of the corporation

Subscribed and Sworn to before me on _____ , 19 ___ .

_____
Notary Public in and for the County of _____ and the
State of _____ . My commission expires
_____ .

Waiver of Notice of First Board of Directors Meeting of _____

We, the undersigned Incorporators of this corporation, waive any required notice and consent to the holding of the first meeting of the board of directors of this corporation on _____ , 19 ___ , at _____ m., at the offices of the corporation, located at

_____

_____ .

Dated _____

Name   Signature

_____   _____

_____   _____

_____   _____

_____   _____

_____   _____

Minutes of the First Board of Directors Meeting of _____

The first meeting of the board of directors of this corporation was held on
_____ , 19 ___ , at _____ m.,
at _____ .

Present at the meeting were the following people:

_____
_____ , all of whom
are designated as directors of this corporation in the Articles of Incorporation.

The following other persons were also present

_____
_____ .

1. _____ was elected as the
   temporary Chairperson of the board.

   _____ was elected as the
   temporary Secretary of the board.

2. The Chairperson announced that the meeting had been duly called by the Incorporators of the corporation, called the meeting to order, and determined that a quorum was present.

3. The Secretary then presented an Affidavit of Mailing of Notice or a Waiver of Notice of the meeting which was signed by all directors.

   Upon motion made and carried, the Secretary was ordered to attach the Affidavit of Notice or the Waiver of Notice to the minutes of this meeting.

4. The Chairperson reported that the Articles of Incorporation had been duly filed with the State of _____ on _____ , 19 ___ , and that the incorporation was effective as of _____ , 19 ___ .

   Upon motion made and carried, a copy of the Articles of Incorporation were ordered to be attached to the minutes of this meeting.

5. Upon motion made and carried, the board of directors RESOLVED that:

   The joint and individual acts of _____ and _____ , the incorporators of this corporation, which were taken on behalf of the corporation are approved, ratified, and adopted as acts of the corporation.

6. The following persons were elected as officers of the corporation to serve until the first annual board of directors meeting:

   _____ , President;

   _____ , Vice-President;

   _____ , Treasurer;

   _____ , Secretary.

7. Upon motion made and carried, the annual salaries of the officers were fixed at the following rates until the next annual meeting of the board of directors:

   President $_____ ;

   Vice-President $_____ ;

   Secretary $_____ ;

   Treasurer $_____ .

8. Upon motion made and carried, the board of directors RESOLVED that:

   The officers of this corporation are authorized and directed to pay all fees and expenses necessary for the organization of this corporation. The officers are also directed to procure and prepare the necessary books for corporate accounting.

9. Upon motion made and carried, the board of directors RESOLVED that:

The officers of this corporation be authorized and directed to open a bank account with _____ located at _____ and to deposit all funds of the corporation into this account, with checks payable upon the corporate signature of _____ only.

Further RESOLVED that the officers of this corporation are authorized to execute any formal Bank Resolutions and documents which may be necessary to open such an account. A copy of the formal Bank Resolution for opening this account is hereby adopted and ordered to be attached to the minutes of this meeting.

10. A proposed corporate Seal, corporate Stock Certificate, and Corporate Stock Transfer Book were presented.

Upon motion made and carried, the board of directors RESOLVED that:

The Seal, Stock Certificates, and Stock Transfer Book presented at this meeting are adopted and approved as the Seal, Stock Certificates, and Stock Transfer Book of this corporation. A specimen copy of the Stock Certificate is ordered to be attached to the minutes of this meeting.

11. A copy of the proposed By-Laws of the corporation was presented at the meeting and read by each director.

Upon motion made and carried, the board of directors RESOLVED that:

The proposed By-Laws of this corporation are approved and adopted. A copy of these By-Laws are ordered to be attached to the minutes of this meeting.

12. The following persons have offered to transfer the property or money listed below to the corporation in exchange for the following number of shares of common capital stock in the corporation:

Name	Property or Money	# Shares
_____	_____	_____
_____	_____	_____
_____	_____	_____
_____	_____	_____

Upon motion made and carried, the board of directors RESOLVED that:

The assets proposed for transfer are good and sufficient consideration and the officers are directed to accept the assets on behalf of the corporation and to issue and deliver the appropriate number of shares of stock in this corporation to the respective persons. The shares of stock issued shall be fully-paid and non-assessable common capital stock of this corporation.

13. Upon motion made and carried, the board of directors RESOLVED that:

The fiscal year of this corporation shall begin on _____ and end on _____ . This corporation shall report its income and expenses on a(n)_____ basis.

14. The following other business was conducted:

There being no further business, upon motion made and carried, the meeting was adjourned.

Dated _____

Seal

_____
Secretary of the corporation

Annual Directors Meeting Checklist

The following information should be covered and documented in the minutes of the annual board of directors meeting:

- ❏ Name of corporation
- ❏ State of incorporation
- ❏ Date of meeting
- ❏ Location of meeting
- ❏ Notification of meeting
  - ❏ Notices sent and affidavit filed / or waivers filed
- ❏ Officers present at meeting
- ❏ Others present at meeting
- ❏ Officers presiding over meeting
- ❏ Meeting called to order and quorum present

Annual matters:

- ❏ Date last state corporate tax return filed
- ❏ Date last federal corporate tax return filed
- ❏ Date last state annual report filed
- ❏ Date last federal pension/profit-sharing returns filed
- ❏ Date any other required reports/returns filed
- ❏ Date of last financial statement

- ❏ Review current employment agreements

- ❏ Review current insurance coverage

- ❏ Review stock transfer ledger

- ❏ Review current Financial Statement

    - ❏ Review current year-to-date income and expenses

    - ❏ Review current salaries

    - ❏ Review current pension/profit-sharing plans

    - ❏ Review other employee fringe benefit plans

    - ❏ Review accounts receivable

        - ❏ Determine if collection procedures are warranted

    - ❏ Review status of any outstanding loans

    - ❏ Ascertain net profit

    - ❏ Determine if a stock dividend should be declared

    - ❏ Discuss any major items requiring board action:

        - ❏ Major purchases or leases (real estate or personal property)

        - ❏ Lawsuits

        - ❏ Loans

- ❏ Adjournment of meeting

- ❏ Date and Secretary signature on minutes

Notice of Annual Board of Directors
Meeting of _____

TO:

In accordance with the By-Laws of this corporation, an official regular meeting of the board of directors will be held at _____ m., on _____ , 19 ___ , at the offices of the corporation located at _____
_____.

Dated _____

                                                            Seal

_____
Secretary of the corporation

Affidavit of Mailing of Notice of Annual Board of Directors Meeting of _____

State of _____)
)
County of _____)

Being duly sworn, _____ states:

I am the Secretary of _____ , a
corporation organized under the laws of the State of _____ .

On _____ , 19 ___ , I personally deposited stamped and
sealed copies of Notice of the Annual Directors Meeting of this
corporation in a post-office box in the City of _____ , in
the State of _____ .

The copies were correctly addressed to the following persons:

Name   Address

_____   _____

_____   _____

_____   _____

_____
Secretary of the corporation

Subscribed and Sworn to before me on _____ , 19 ___ .

_____
Notary Public in and for the County of _____ and the
State of _____ . My commission expires _____ .

Waiver of Notice of Annual Board of Directors Meeting of _____

We, the undersigned directors of this corporation, waive any required notice and consent to the holding of the annual meeting of the board of directors of this corporation on _____ , 19 ___ , at _____ m., at the offices of the corporation, located at

_____

_____ .

Dated _____

Name   Signature

_____   _____

_____   _____

_____   _____

_____   _____

_____   _____

_____   _____

Minutes of the Annual Board of Directors Meeting of _____

The annual meeting of the board of directors of this corporation was held on _____ , 19 ___ , at _____ m., at _____ .

Present at the meeting were the following people:

_____

_____ ,

all of whom are directors of this corporation.

Present also were the following people:

_____

_____ .

_____ , the President of the corporation presided over the meeting.

_____ , the Secretary of the corporation served as secretary for the meeting.

1. The President called the meeting to order. The President determined that a quorum was present and that the meeting could conduct business.

2. The Secretary reported that notice of the meeting had been properly given or waived by each Director in accordance with the By-Laws.

    Upon motion made and carried, the Secretary was directed to attach the appropriate Notice and Affidavit or Waiver to these minutes.

3. The Secretary distributed copies of the minutes of the previous meeting of the board of directors which had been held on _____ , 19 ___ .

    Upon motion made and carried, these minutes were approved.

4. The President presented the annual President's Report.

Upon motion made and carried, the President's Report was approved and the Secretary was directed to attach a copy of the President's Report to these minutes.

5. The Treasurer of the corporation, presented the Treasurer's Report, which stated that as of _____ , 19 ___ , the corporation had a net profit of $_____ .

    Upon motion made and carried, the Treasurer's Report was approved and the Secretary was directed to attach a copy of the Treasurer's Report to these minutes.

6. Upon motion made and carried, the board of directors RESOLVED that:

    A dividend of $_____ per share of common stock is declared on the stock of this corporation. This dividend shall be paid to the shareholders of record as of _____ , 19 ___ and shall be paid on _____ , 19 ___ . The officers of this corporation are directed to take all necessary actions to carry out this resolution.

7. Upon motion made and carried, the following persons were elected as officers of this corporation for a term of one year:

    _____ , President;

    _____ , Vice President;

    _____ , Treasurer;

    _____ , Secretary.

8. Upon motion made and carried, the salaries of the officers were fixed for the term of one year at the following rates:

    President $_____

    Vice-President $_____

    Secretary $_____

    Treasurer $_____

9.   The following other business was transacted:

        There being no further business, upon motion made and carried, the meeting was adjourned.

Dated _____

                                                    Seal

_____
Secretary of the corporation

Special Directors Meeting Checklist

The following information should be covered and documented in the minutes of any special board of directors meeting:

- ❏ Name of corporation
- ❏ State of incorporation
- ❏ Date of meeting
- ❏ Location of meeting
- ❏ Specific purpose of meeting
- ❏ Proper notification of meeting
  - ❏ Notices sent and affidavit filed / or waivers filed
- ❏ Officers present at meeting
- ❏ Others present at meeting
- ❏ Name of President presiding over meeting
- ❏ Name of Secretary acting at meeting
- ❏ Meeting called to order and quorum present

Business Transacted:

- ❏ Specific business discussed at meeting
- ❏ Resolutions passed at meeting
- ❏ Adjournment of meeting
- ❏ Date and Secretary signature on minutes

Notice of Special Board of Directors Meeting of _____

TO:

In accordance with the By-Laws of this corporation, a special meeting of the board of directors will be held at _____ m., on _____ , 19 ___ , at the offices of the corporation located at _____ _____.

The purpose of this special meeting will be to discuss and take any required action regarding the following matter:

Dated _____

Seal

_____
Secretary of the corporation

Affidavit of Mailing of Notice of Special Board of Directors Meeting of _____

State of _____   )
)
County of _____   )

Being duly sworn, _____ states:
I am the Secretary of _____ , a
corporation organized under the laws of the State of _____ .

On _____ , 19 ___ , I personally deposited stamped and
sealed copies of Notice of the Special Directors Meeting of this
corporation in a post-office box in the City of _____ , in
the State of _____ . The copies were correctly addressed
to the following persons:

Name   Address

_____   _____

_____   _____

_____   _____

_____
Secretary of the corporation

Subscribed and Sworn to before me on _____ , 19 ___ .

_____
Notary Public in and for the County of _____ and the
State of _____ . My commission expires
_____ .

Waiver of Notice of Special Board of Directors Meeting of _____

We, the undersigned directors of this corporation waive any required notice and consent to the holding of a special meeting of the board of directors of this corporation on _____ , 19 ___ , at _____ m., at the offices of the corporation, located at

_____

_____ .

Dated _____

Name	Signature
_____	_____
_____	_____
_____	_____
_____	_____
_____	_____
_____	_____

Minutes of Special Board of Directors
Meeting of _____

A special meeting of the board of directors of this corporation was held on _____ , 19 ___ , at _____ m., at _____ .

The purpose of this special meeting was: _____
_____ .

Present at the meeting were the following people:
_____
_____ ,
all of whom are directors of this corporation.

Present also were the following people: _____
_____ .

_____ , the President of the corporation presided over the meeting.

_____ , the Secretary of the corporation served as secretary for the meeting.

1. The President called the meeting to order. The President determined that a quorum was present and that the meeting could conduct business.

2. The Secretary reported that notice of the meeting had been properly given or waived by each Director in accordance with the By-Laws.

    Upon motion made and carried, the Secretary was directed to attach the appropriate Notice and Affidavit or Waiver to these minutes.

3. The following business was then discussed:

4. Upon motion made and carried, the board of directors RESOLVED that:

There being no further business, upon motion made and carried, the meeting was adjourned.

Dated _____

Seal

_____
Secretary of the corporation

Chapter 9

Corporate Shareholders Meetings

The main responsibility of the shareholders of a corporation is to elect the directors of the business. This election is conducted at the annual meeting of the shareholders which is held on the date, time, and place as specified in the corporate By-Laws. In addition, specific corporate business at other times of the year may occasionally need shareholder approval. For example, shareholders must vote on the dissolution of the corporation (see Chapter 15), on amendments to the By-Laws or Articles of Incorporation (see Chapter 7), and on any extraordinary business transactions, such as the sale of all of the assets of the corporation. For these purposes, a special meeting of the shareholders must be held.

The initial meeting of the shareholders also has a slightly different agenda. At this meeting, the shareholders approve and ratify the adoption of the corporate By-Laws, and ratify the election or appointment of the initial board of directors who will serve until the first annual meeting of the shareholders. The shareholders also approve the election of the first officers of the corporation by the board of directors.

On the following pages, there are Checklists and forms for the initial, annual, and special shareholders meetings. Please follow the Checklists in preparing the forms. The notice requirements for shareholders meetings are identical to those for directors meetings. However, the forms are slightly different.

First Shareholders Meeting Checklist

The following information should be covered and documented in the minutes of the first shareholders meeting:

☐ Name of corporation

☐ Date of meeting

☐ Location of meeting

☐ Officers present at meeting

☐ Others present at meeting

☐ Meeting called to order and quorum present

☐ Shareholders present at meeting

☐ Shareholders represented by proxy at meeting

☐ Name of President acting at meeting

☐ Name of Secretary acting at meeting

☐ Name of Chairperson elected to preside over meeting

☐ Proper notification of meeting

    ☐ Notice sent and affidavit filed / or waivers filed

☐ Minutes of first directors meeting read

☐ Minutes of first directors meeting approved and ratified

☐ Election of directors and officers approved and ratified

☐ Adoption of corporate By-Laws approved and ratified

❐ Any other business

❐ Meeting adjourned

❐ Secretary dated and signed minutes

Notice of First Shareholders Meeting of _____

TO:

In accordance with the By-Laws of this corporation, a first official meeting of the shareholders will be held at _____ m., on _____ , 19 ___ , at the offices of the corporation located at _____ _____ .

The purpose of this meeting is to approve adoption of the By-Laws of this corporation, approve election of the officers, approve continuation of the directors of this corporation, and to transact any other necessary business.

The Stock Transfer Book of this corporation will remain closed from _____ , 19 ___ until _____ , 19 ___ .

Dated _____

Seal

_____
Secretary of the corporation

Affidavit of Mailing of Notice of First Shareholders Meeting of _____

State of _____)
)
County of _____)

Being duly sworn, _____ states:
I am the Secretary of _____ , a
corporation organized under the laws of the State of _____ .

On _____ , 19 ___ , I personally deposited stamped and
sealed copies of Notice of the First Shareholders Meeting of this
corporation in a post-office box in the City of _____ , in
the State of _____ .

The copies were correctly addressed to all shareholders of this
corporation as of _____ , 19 ___ , as shown in the Stock
Transfer Book of this corporation. The list of names and addresses of the
shareholders is attached to this Affidavit.

_____
Secretary of the corporation

Subscribed and Sworn to before me on _____ , 19 ___ .

_____
Notary Public in and for the County of _____ and the
State of _____ . My commission expires _____ .

Waiver of Notice of First Shareholders Meeting
of _____

We, the undersigned shareholders of this corporation, waive any required notice and consent to the holding of the first meeting of the shareholders of this corporation on _____ , 19 ___ , at _____ m., at the offices of the corporation, located at _____ _____ .

Dated _____

Name   Signature

_____   _____

_____   _____

_____   _____

_____   _____

_____   _____

_____   _____

_____   _____

Authorization to Vote Shares (PROXY) _____

I, _____ , the record owner of
this corporation's stock certificate # _____ , which
represents _____ shares in this corporation, authorize
_____ to vote all of these shares
at the meeting of the shareholders of this corporation which is scheduled
to be held on _____ , 19 ___ at _____ m.
at the offices of this corporation, which are located at: _____
_____ .

Through the use of this proxy and authorization, _____ ,
has the right to vote these shares at any business conducted at this
meeting as if I personally were present.

This proxy and authorization may be revoked by me at any time prior to
the meeting and will be void if I personally attend the meeting.

Dated _____

_____
Name of Shareholder

_____
Signature of Shareholder

Minutes of the First Shareholders Meeting of _____

The first meeting of the shareholders of this corporation was held on
_____ , 19 ___ , at _____ m.,
at _____ .

The President of this corporation, _____,
and the Vice-President of this corporation, _____,
and the Secretary of this corporation, _____,
and the Treasurer of this corporation, _____,
were present.

Other than shareholders of this corporation, the following other persons
were also present _____

_____ .

1. The President of this corporation called the meeting to order and
    determined that a quorum was present, either in person or by
    proxy.

    The following shareholders were present in person:

    Name   Number of shares

    _____   _____

    _____   _____

    _____   _____

    _____   _____

    _____   _____

    _____   _____

    _____   _____

    _____   _____

The following shareholders were represented by proxy:

Name   Number of shares

_____   _____

_____   _____

_____   _____

_____   _____

_____   _____

2. The Secretary of this corporation reported that notice of the meeting had been properly given or waived by each shareholder in accordance with the By-Laws.

Upon motion made and carried, the Secretary was directed to attach the appropriate Notice and Affidavit or Waiver to these minutes.

3. _____ was then elected Chairperson of this meeting.

4. The Secretary read the minutes of the first meeting of the board of directors of this corporation which was held on _____, 19 ___.

Upon motion made and carried, the shareholders RESOLVED that:

All acts taken and decisions made at the first meeting of the board of directors of this corporation are approved and ratified, specifically that the shareholders approve and ratify the adoption of the By-Laws of this corporation and that the shareholders approve and ratify the election of the following persons as officers for the terms as stated in the minutes of the first meeting of the board of directors:

_____ , President;

_____ , Vice-President;

_____ , Treasurer;

_____ , Secretary;

5. Upon motion made and carried, the shareholders RESOLVED that:

    The following persons are designated as the initial directors of this corporation in the Articles of Incorporation and the shareholders approve and ratify this designation of the following persons as directors of this corporation until the first annual meeting of the shareholders of this corporation:

    _____ , Director;

    _____ , Director;

    _____ , Director.

6. The following other business was transacted:

    There being no further business, upon motion made and carried, the meeting was adjourned.

Dated _____

                                                Seal

_____
Secretary of the corporation

Annual Shareholders Meeting Checklist

The following information should be covered and documented in the minutes of the annual shareholders meetings:

☐ Name of corporation

☐ Date of meeting

☐ Location of meeting

☐ Officers present at meeting

☐ Others present at meeting

☐ Meeting called to order and quorum present

☐ Shareholders present at meeting

☐ Shareholders represented by proxy at meeting

☐ Name of President acting at meeting

☐ Name of Secretary acting at meeting

☐ Name of Chairperson elected to preside over meeting

☐ Proper notification of meeting

☐ Notices sent and affidavit filed / or waivers filed

☐ Minutes of previous shareholders meeting read

☐ Minutes of previous shareholders meeting approved

☐ Presidents report read and approved and directed to be attached to minutes

- ❏ Treasurers report read and approved and directed to be attached to minutes

- ❏ Nomination of persons to serve as directors

- ❏ Election of directors

- ❏ Any other business

- ❏ Meeting adjourned

- ❏ Secretary dated and signed minutes

Notice of Annual Shareholders Meeting of _____

TO:

In accordance with the By-Laws of this corporation, an official annual meeting of the shareholders will be held at _____ m., on _____ , 19 ___ , at the offices of the corporation located at _____.

The purpose of this meeting is to elect directors of this corporation and to transact any other necessary business.

The Stock Transfer Book of this corporation will remain closed from _____ , 19 ___ until _____ , 19 ___.

Dated _____

                                                    Seal

_____
Secretary of the corporation

Affidavit of Mailing of Notice of Annual Shareholders Meeting of _____

State of _____   )
)
County of _____   )

Being duly sworn, _____ states:

I am the Secretary of _____ , a corporation organized under the laws of the State of
_____ .

On _____ , 19 ___ , I personally deposited stamped and sealed copies of Notice of the Annual Shareholders Meeting of this corporation in a post-office box in the City of _____ , in the State of _____ .

The copies were correctly addressed to all shareholders of this corporation as of _____ , 19 ___ as shown in the Stock Transfer Book of this corporation. The list of names and addresses of the shareholders is attached to this Affidavit.

_____
Secretary of the corporation

Subscribed and Sworn to before me on _____ , 19 ___ .

_____
Notary Public in and for the County of _____ and the
State of _____ . My commission expires _____ .

Waiver of Notice of Annual Shareholders Meeting of _____

We, the undersigned shareholders of this corporation, waive any required notice and consent to the holding of the annual meeting of the shareholders of this corporation on _____ , 19 ___ , at _____ m., at the offices of the corporation, located at

_____

_____ .

Dated _____

Name   Signature

_____   _____

_____   _____

_____   _____

_____   _____

_____   _____

_____   _____

Minutes of the Annual Shareholders Meeting of _____

The annual meeting of the shareholders of this corporation was held on
_____ , 19 ___ , at
_____ m., at _____
_____.

The President of this corporation, _____,
and the Vice-President of this corporation, _____,
and the Secretary of this corporation, _____,
and the Treasurer of this corporation, _____,
were present.

Other than shareholders, the following other persons were also present
_____
_____.

1. The President of this corporation called the meeting to order and
    determined that a quorum was present, either in person or by
    proxy.

    The following shareholders were present in person:

    Name   Number of Shares

    _____   _____

    _____   _____

    _____   _____

    _____   _____

    _____   _____

    _____   _____

    _____   _____

The following shareholders were represented by proxy:

Name   Number of Shares

_____   _____

_____   _____

_____   _____

_____   _____

_____   _____

2.   The Secretary of this corporation reported that notice of the meeting had been properly given or waived by each shareholder in accordance with the By-Laws.

Upon motion made and carried, the Secretary was directed to attach the appropriate Notice and Affidavit or Waiver to these minutes.

3.   _____ was then elected Chairperson of this meeting.

4.   The Secretary distributed copies of the minutes of the previous meeting of the shareholders which had been held on _____, 19 ___ .

Upon motion made and carried, these minutes were approved.

4.   The President presented the annual President's Report.

Upon motion made and carried, the President's Report was approved and the Secretary was directed to attach a copy of the President's Report to these minutes.

5.   The Treasurer of the corporation presented the Treasurer's Report.

Upon motion made and carried, the Treasurer's Report was approved and the Secretary was directed to attach a copy of the Treasurer's Report to these minutes.

6. The following persons were nominated as directors of this
    corporation for a term of _____ year(s):
    Name

    _____

    _____

    _____

    _____

7. In accordance with the By-Laws of this corporation, an election of
    directors was held, with each shareholder stating their choices for
    director by secret ballot and the number of shares held personally
    or by proxy.

8. The votes were tallied by the Secretary and, by a majority vote of
    the outstanding shares entitled to vote in this election, the following
    persons were elected as directors of this corporation for a term of
    _____ year(s):

    _____ ;

    _____ ;

    _____ .

9. On motion made and carried, it was directed that a report of the
    election be filed with the Clerk of _____ County,
    State of _____ , if required.

10. The following other business was transacted:

    There being no further business, upon motion made and carried the
    meeting was adjourned.

Dated _____

                                        Seal

_____
Secretary of the corporation

Special Shareholders Meeting Checklist

The following information should be covered and documented in the minutes of any special shareholders meetings:

- ❏ Name of corporation

- ❏ Date of meeting

- ❏ Location of meeting

- ❏ Officers present at meeting

- ❏ Others present at meeting

- ❏ Meeting called to order and quorum present

- ❏ Shareholders present at meeting

- ❏ Shareholders represented by proxy at meeting

- ❏ Name of President acting at meeting

- ❏ Name of Secretary acting at meeting

- ❏ Name of Chairperson elected to preside over meeting

- ❏ Proper notification of meeting

  - ❏ Notices sent and affidavit filed / or waivers filed

- ❏ Specific business discussed

- ❏ Specific shareholders resolutions adopted

- ❏ Meeting adjourned

- ❏ Secretary dated and signed minutes

Notice of Special Shareholders Meeting of _____

TO:

In accordance with the By-Laws of this corporation, an official special meeting of the shareholders will be held at _____ m., on _____ , 19 ___ , at the offices of the corporation located at _____ .

The purpose of this meeting is the following:

The Stock Transfer Book of this corporation will remain closed from _____ , 19 ___ until _____ , 19 ___ .

Dated _____

Seal

_____
Secretary of the corporation

Affidavit of Mailing of Notice of Special Shareholders Meeting of _____

State of _____   )
)   S.S.
County of _____   )

Being duly sworn, _____ states:

I am the Secretary of _____ , a corporation organized under the laws of the State of

_____ .

On _____ , 19 ___ , I personally deposited stamped and sealed copies of Notice of the Special Shareholders Meeting of this corporation in a post-office box in the City of _____ , in the State of _____ .

The copies were correctly addressed to all shareholders of this corporation as of _____ , 19 ___ as shown in the Stock Transfer Book of this corporation. The list of names and addresses of the shareholders is attached to this Affidavit.

_____
Secretary of the corporation

Subscribed and Sworn to before me on _____ , 19 ___ .

_____
Notary Public in and for the County of _____ and the
State of _____ . My commission expires _____ .

Waiver of Notice of Special Shareholders Meeting of _____

We, the undersigned shareholders of this corporation, waive any required notice and consent to the holding of the special meeting of the shareholders of this corporation on _____ , 19 ___ , at _____ m., at the offices of the corporation, located at

_____

_____.

Dated _____

Name   Signature

_____   _____

_____   _____

_____   _____

_____   _____

_____   _____

_____   _____

_____   _____

_____   _____

Minutes of the Special Shareholders Meeting of _____

A special meeting of the shareholders of this corporation was held on
_____ , 19 ___ , at _____ m.,
at the offices of the corporation located at

_____
_____ .

The President of this corporation, _____,
and the Vice-President of this corporation, _____,
and the Secretary of this corporation, _____,
and the Treasurer of this corporation, _____,
were present.

Other than shareholders, the following other persons were also present

_____
_____ .

1.   The President of this corporation called the meeting to order and
     determined that a quorum was present, either in person or by
     proxy.

     The following shareholders were present in person:

     Name   Number of Shares

     _____   _____

     _____   _____

     _____   _____

     _____   _____

     _____   _____

     _____   _____

     _____   _____

The following shareholders were represented by proxy:

Name   Number of Shares

_____   _____

_____   _____

_____   _____

2. The Secretary of this corporation reported that notice of the meeting had been properly given or waived by each shareholder in accordance with the By-Laws.

    Upon motion made and carried, the Secretary was directed to attach the appropriate Notice and Affidavit or Waiver to these minutes.

3. _____ was then elected Chairperson of this meeting.

4. The following business was discussed:

5. Upon motion made and carried, the following resolution was approved by a majority of the outstanding shares entitled to vote on this measure:
    RESOLVED that:

6. The President declared that this shareholders resolution was duly adopted.

There being no further business, upon motion made and carried, the meeting was adjourned.

Dated _____

                                        Seal

_____
Secretary of the corporation

Chapter 10

Corporate Resolutions

Corporate resolutions are records of official acts of either the shareholders of the corporation or the board of directors. They are a permanent record of actions taken by either of these bodies as a group. In most situations and for most corporations, a majority vote of the directors or shareholders present at an official meeting (as long as the number present constitutes a quorum) is required to adopt a corporate resolution. The resolutions adopted should be kept permanently in the corporate record book. In some cases, a copy of the resolution will be required by a third party. For example, a financial institution will usually require a copy of the corporate resolution which authorizes an officer to bind the corporation in a loan transaction.

Two Checklists follow which specify the general circumstances in which corporate resolutions are required. They are not required for all of the normal day-to-day transactions of a business. In general, directors resolutions are only necessary to document the major decisions or transactions of a corporation. Shareholders resolutions are even more rare, used only for extraordinary corporate matters.

In recent years, the use of consent resolutions has increased among businesses. These resolutions are used in lieu of formal meetings and can simplify corporate management. They require, however, the written consent of all of the directors (or shareholders) of a corporation in order to be valid. Any of the resolutions in this chapter can be used as consent resolutions by adapting them using the Consent Resolution instructions located at the end of this chapter.

Corporate Resolutions Checklists

Formal corporate resolutions are generally required in the following circumstances. Most sample directors resolutions are contained in this chapter. Additional directors and shareholders resolutions relating to amendments to the Articles of Incorporation and amendments to By-Laws are contained in Chapter 7. Resolutions relating to the dissolution of a corporation are found in Chapter 15.

Directors resolutions:

❑ Authorizing of major contracts

❑ Authorizing the sale of corporate real estate

❑ Authorizing the purchase of real estate

❑ Authorizing the corporation to borrow money

❑ Authorizing the corporation to enter into a real estate lease

❑ Authorizing a lawsuit

❑ Authorizing the appointment of a lawyer

❑ Authorizing the appointment of an accountant

❑ Authorizing stock dividends

❑ Authorizing stock dividends to be declared and paid annually

❑ Authorizing stock dividends to be declared and paid quarterly

❑ Authorizing the reimbursement of expenses to an employee

❑ Authorizing the retention of corporate earnings

❑ Authorizing employee stock option plans

❑ Authorizing pension plans

- ❐ Authorizing profit-sharing plans
- ❐ Authorizing health care plans
- ❐ Authorizing group insurance plans
- ❐ Authorizing death benefit plans
- ❐ Authorizing other employee benefit plans
- ❐ Authorizing recision of prior resolutions
- ❐ Authorizing loans to directors or officers
- ❐ Authorizing the payment of officer's salaries
- ❐ Authorizing a restricted stock transfer
- ❐ Authorizing a registered office address change
- ❐ Authorizing the corporate president to make purchases
- ❐ Authorizing the payment of a bonus to employees

Shareholders resolutions:

- ❐ Approving the sale of all of the corporate assets
- ❐ Approving the dissolution of the corporation (see Chapter 15)

Resolution of the Board of Directors of _____

A meeting of the board of directors of this corporation was duly called and held on _____ , 19 ___.

A quorum of the board of directors was present and at the meeting it was decided, by majority vote, that

Therefore, it is
RESOLVED, that this corporation

The officers of this corporation are hereby authorized to perform all necessary acts to carry out this resolution.

The undersigned, _____ , certifies that he or she is the duly elected Secretary of this corporation and that the above is a true and correct copy of the resolution that was duly adopted at a meeting of the board of directors which was held in accordance with state law and the By-Laws of the corporation on _____ , 19 ___ .

I further certify that such resolution is now in full force and effect.

Dated _____

Seal

_____
Secretary of the corporation

Resolution of the Board of Directors
of _____ Authorizing Contract

A meeting of the board of directors of this corporation was duly called and held on _____ , 19 ___.

A quorum of the board of directors was present and at the meeting it was decided, by majority vote, that it is necessary for the corporation to enter into a contract with _____ of _____ for the following purpose:

Therefore, it is
RESOLVED, that this corporation enter into a contract with _____ of _____ for the stated purpose. The officers of this corporation are hereby authorized to perform all necessary acts to carry out this resolution.

The undersigned, _____ ,
certifies that he or she is the duly elected Secretary of this corporation and that the above is a true and correct copy of the resolution that was duly adopted at a meeting of the board of directors which was held in accordance with state law and the By-Laws of the corporation on _____ , 19 ___.

I further certify that such resolution is now in full force and effect.

Dated _____

Seal

_____
Secretary of the corporation

Resolution of the Board of Directors of _____ Authorizing Sale of Real Estate

A meeting of the board of directors of this corporation was duly called and held on _____ , 19 ___.

A quorum of the board of directors was present and at the meeting it was decided, by majority vote, that it has become necessary, for the benefit of the corporation, to sell the real estate described as follows:

Therefore, it is
RESOLVED, that the corporation sell the real estate described as

to _____ of _____
for the price of $_____ . The officers of this corporation
are hereby authorized to perform all necessary acts to carry out such sale.

The undersigned, _____ ,
certifies that he or she is the duly elected Secretary of this corporation and that the above is a true and correct copy of the resolution that was duly adopted at a meeting of the board of directors which was held in accordance with state law and the By-Laws of the corporation on _____ , 19 ___.

I further certify that such resolution is now in full force and effect.

Dated _____

Seal

_____
Secretary of the corporation

Resolution of the Board of Directors of _____ Authorizing Purchase of Real Estate

A meeting of the board of directors of this corporation was duly called and held on _____ , 19 ___.

A quorum of the board of directors was present and at the meeting it was decided, by majority vote, that it has become necessary for the corporation to purchase the real estate described as follows:

Therefore, it is
RESOLVED, that the corporation purchase the real estate described as:

from _____ of _____
for the price of $ _____ . The officers of this corporation are hereby authorized to perform all necessary acts to carry out such purchase.

The undersigned, _____ _____ ,
certifies that he or she is the duly elected Secretary of this corporation and that the above is a true and correct copy of the resolution that was duly adopted at a meeting of the board of directors which was held in accordance with state law and the By-Laws of the corporation on
_____ , 19 ___.

I further certify that such resolution is now in full force and effect.

Dated _____

Seal

_____
Secretary of the corporation

Resolution of the Board of Directors of _____
Authorizing Borrowing Money

A meeting of the board of directors of this corporation was duly called and held on _____ , 19 ___.

A quorum of the board of directors was present and at the meeting it was decided, by majority vote, that it has become necessary for the corporation to borrow money for the purpose of:

Therefore, it is
RESOLVED, that this corporation borrow $_____ from
_____ of _____
on the following terms:

The officers of this corporation are hereby authorized to perform all necessary acts to carry out such transaction.

The undersigned, _____ ,
certifies that he or she is the duly elected Secretary of this corporation and that the above is a true and correct copy of the resolution that was duly adopted at a meeting of the board of directors which was held in accordance with state law and the By-Laws of the corporation on
_____ , 19 ___.

I further certify that such resolution is now in full force and effect.

Dated _____

                                        Seal

_____
Secretary of the corporation

Resolution of the Board of Directors of _____ Authorizing Lease

A meeting of the board of directors of this corporation was duly called and held on _____ , 19 ___ .

A quorum of the board of directors was present and at the meeting it was decided, by majority vote, that it has become necessary to enter into a lease of the real estate located at:

Therefore, it is
RESOLVED, that this corporation enter into a lease for the period from
_____ , 19 ___ to _____ , 19 ___ with _____ of _____ for the real estate located at:

The lease payments shall be $_____ each
_____ .

The officers of this corporation are hereby authorized to perform all necessary acts to enter into such lease.

The undersigned, _____ , certifies that he or she is the duly elected Secretary of this corporation and that the above is a true and correct copy of the resolution that was duly adopted at a meeting of the board of directors which was held in accordance with state law and the By-Laws of the corporation on _____ , 19 ___ .

I further certify that such resolution is now in full force and effect.

Dated _____

_____   Seal

_____
Secretary of the corporation

Resolution of the Board of Directors of _____ Authorizing Lawsuit

A meeting of the board of directors of this corporation was duly called and held on _____ , 19 ___.

A quorum of the board of directors was present and at the meeting it was decided, by majority vote, that it has become necessary to file a lawsuit against _____ for the purpose of:

Therefore, it is
RESOLVED, that this corporation file a lawsuit in the jurisdiction of _____ against _____
of _____ on the grounds of:

The officers of this corporation are hereby authorized to perform all necessary acts to carry out this resolution.

The undersigned, _____ ,
certifies that he or she is the duly elected Secretary of this corporation and that the above is a true and correct copy of the resolution that was duly adopted at a meeting of the board of directors which was held in accordance with state law and the By-Laws of the corporation on _____ , 19 ___.

I further certify that such resolution is now in full force and effect.

Dated _____

                                                        Seal

_____
Secretary of the corporation

Resolution of the Board of Directors of _____ Authorizing Appointment of Lawyer

A meeting of the board of directors of this corporation was duly called and held on _____ , 19 ___.

A quorum of the board of directors was present and at the meeting it was decided, by majority vote, that it has become necessary to appoint a lawyer for the purpose of:

Therefore, it is
RESOLVED, that this corporation appoint
_____ of _____
to represent the corporation in the following matter:

The officers of this corporation are hereby authorized to perform all necessary acts to carry out this resolution.

The undersigned, _____ ,
certifies that he or she is the duly elected Secretary of this corporation and that the above is a true and correct copy of the resolution that was duly adopted at a meeting of the board of directors which was held in accordance with state law and the By-Laws of the corporation on
_____ , 19 ___.

I further certify that such resolution is now in full force and effect.

Dated _____

Seal

_____
Secretary of the corporation

Resolution of the Board of Directors of _____ Appointing Accountant

A meeting of the board of directors of this corporation was duly called and held on _____ , 19 ___ .

A quorum of the board of directors was present and at the meeting it was decided, by majority vote, that it has become necessary to appoint an accountant for the purpose of:

Therefore, it is
RESOLVED, that this corporation appoint
_____ of _____
in the following matter:

The officers of this corporation are hereby authorized to perform all necessary acts to carry out this resolution.

The undersigned, _____ ,
certifies that he or she is the duly elected Secretary of this corporation and that the above is a true and correct copy of the resolution that was duly adopted at a meeting of the board of directors which was held in accordance with state law and the By-Laws of the corporation on
_____ , 19 ___ .

I further certify that such resolution is now in full force and effect.

Dated _____

Seal

_____
Secretary of the corporation

Resolution of the Board of Directors of _____ Authorizing Stock Dividend

A meeting of the board of directors of this corporation was duly called and held on _____ , 19 ___.

A quorum of the board of directors was present and at the meeting it was decided, by majority vote, that since the corporation has $_____ of undistributed surplus funds, $_____ should be distributed as a stock dividend.

Therefore, it is
RESOLVED, that this corporation declares a stock dividend in the amount of $_____ per share of common stock and that this dividend be paid to the stockholders of record as of _____ , 19 ___ , and that the dividend by paid on _____ , 19 ___.

The officers of this corporation are hereby authorized to perform all necessary acts to carry out this resolution.

The undersigned, _____ , certifies that he or she is the duly elected Secretary of this corporation and that the above is a true and correct copy of the resolution that was duly adopted at a meeting of the board of directors which was held in accordance with state law and the By-Laws of the corporation on _____ , 19 ___.

I further certify that such resolution is now in full force and effect.

Dated _____

Seal

_____
Secretary of the corporation

Resolution of the Board of Directors of _____ Authorizing Annual Dividends

A meeting of the board of directors of this corporation was duly called and held on _____ , 19 ___.

A quorum of the board of directors was present and at the meeting it was decided, by majority vote, that the corporation pay an annual dividend of $_____ per share of common stock, payable on _____ of each year.

Therefore, it is
RESOLVED, that this corporation pay an annual dividend of $_____ per share of common stock, providing its earnings should warrant. This dividend shall be payable on _____ of each year to stockholders of record on _____ of each year.

The officers of this corporation are hereby authorized to perform all necessary acts to carry out this resolution.

The undersigned, _____ , certifies that he or she is the duly elected Secretary of this corporation and that the above is a true and correct copy of the resolution that was duly adopted at a meeting of the board of directors which was held in accordance with state law and the By-Laws of the corporation on _____ , 19 ___.

I further certify that such resolution is now in full force and effect.

Dated _____

Seal

_____
Secretary of the corporation

Resolution of the Board of Directors of _____ Authorizing Quarterly Dividends

A meeting of the board of directors of this corporation was duly called and held on _____ , 19 ___.

A quorum of the board of directors was present and at the meeting it was decided, by majority vote, that the corporation pay a quarterly dividend of $_____ per share of common stock.

Therefore, it is
RESOLVED, that this corporation pay a quarterly dividend of $_____ per share of common stock, providing its earnings should warrant. This dividend shall be payable on _____ , _____ , _____ , and _____ of each year to stockholders of record on _____ , _____ , _____ , and _____ of each year.

The officers of this corporation are hereby authorized to perform all necessary acts to carry out this resolution.

The undersigned, _____ , certifies that he or she is the duly elected Secretary of this corporation and that the above is a true and correct copy of the resolution that was duly adopted at a meeting of the board of directors which was held in accordance with state law and the By-Laws of the corporation on _____ , 19 ___.

I further certify that such resolution is now in full force and effect.

Dated _____

Seal

_____
Secretary of the corporation

Resolution of the Board of Directors of _____ Authorizing Expense Reimbursement

A meeting of the board of directors of this corporation was duly called and held on _____ , 19 ___ .

A quorum of the board of directors was present and at the meeting it was decided, by majority vote, that it is necessary for the benefit of the corporation that the corporation reimburse _____ , who is the _____ of this corporation, for expenses incurred on behalf of the corporation.

Therefore, it is
RESOLVED, that this corporation reimburse
_____ the amount of $ _____
for expenses incurred on behalf of the corporation between the periods of
_____ , 19 ___ and _____ , 19 ___ .

The officers of this corporation are authorized to perform all necessary acts to carry out this resolution.

The undersigned, _____ ,
certifies that he or she is the duly elected Secretary of this corporation and that the above is a true and correct copy of the resolution that was duly adopted at a meeting of the board of directors which was held in accordance with state law and the By-Laws of the corporation on
_____ , 19 ___ .

I further certify that such resolution is now in full force and effect.

Dated _____

Seal

_____
Secretary of the corporation

Resolution of the Board of Directors of _____
Authorizing Retention of Earnings

A meeting of the board of directors of this corporation was duly called and held on _____ , 19 ___.

A quorum of the board of directors was present and at the meeting it was decided, by majority vote, that, to improve the financial condition of the corporation, it is advisable that no dividends be paid and that corporate earnings be retained by the corporation for the fiscal year 19 ___.

Therefore, it is
RESOLVED, that this corporation retain the earnings of the corporation for the fiscal year 19 ___ ; and that such earnings be credited to the corporate Surplus Account; and that no dividends be paid for the fiscal year 19 ___.

The officers of this corporation are authorized to perform all necessary acts to carry out this resolution.

The undersigned, _____ ,
certifies that he or she is the duly elected Secretary of this corporation and that the above is a true and correct copy of the resolution that was duly adopted at a meeting of the board of directors which was held in accordance with state law and the By-Laws of the corporation on
_____ , 19 ___.

I further certify that such resolution is now in full force and effect.

Dated _____

Seal

_____
Secretary of the corporation

Resolution of the Board of Directors of _____ Authorizing Stock Option Plan

A meeting of the board of directors of this corporation was duly called and held on _____ , 19 ___.

A quorum of the board of directors was present and at the meeting it was decided, by majority vote, that it is advisable to provide an employee stock option plan for employees of the corporation.

Therefore, it is
RESOLVED, that this corporation adopts and approves the Employee Stock Option Plan dated _____ , 19 ___ , a copy of which is attached to this resolution and is made a part of the permanent records of this corporation.

The officers of this corporation are authorized to perform all necessary acts to carry out this resolution.

The undersigned, _____ , certifies that he or she is the duly elected Secretary of this corporation and that the above is a true and correct copy of the resolution that was duly adopted at a meeting of the board of directors which was held in accordance with state law and the By-Laws of the corporation on _____ , 19 ___.

I further certify that such resolution is now in full force and effect.

Dated _____

Seal

_____
Secretary of the corporation

Resolution of the Board of Directors of _____ Authorizing Pension Plan

A meeting of the board of directors of this corporation was duly called and held on _____ , 19 ___.

A quorum of the board of directors was present and at the meeting it was decided, by majority vote, that it is advisable that the corporation adopt a pension plan for its employees.

Therefore, it is
RESOLVED, that this corporation adopts and approves the Corporate Pension Plan dated _____ , 19 ___ , a copy of which is attached to this resolution and is made a part of the permanent records of this corporation.

The officers of this corporation are authorized to perform all necessary acts to carry out this resolution.

The undersigned, _____ ,
certifies that he or she is the duly elected Secretary of this corporation and that the above is a true and correct copy of the resolution that was duly adopted at a meeting of the board of directors which was held in accordance with state law and the By-Laws of the corporation on _____ , 19 ___.

I further certify that such resolution is now in full force and effect.

Dated _____

Seal

_____
Secretary of the corporation

Resolution of the Board of Directors of _____
Authorizing Profit-Sharing Plan

A meeting of the board of directors of this corporation was duly called and held on _____ , 19 ___.

A quorum of the board of directors was present and at the meeting it was decided, by majority vote, that it is advisable that the corporation provide its employees with a profit-sharing plan.

Therefore, it is
RESOLVED, that this corporation adopts and approves the Corporate Profit-Sharing Plan dated _____ , 19 ___ , a copy of which is attached to this resolution and which is made a part of the permanent records of this corporation.

The officers of this corporation are authorized to perform all necessary acts to carry out this resolution.

The undersigned, _____ ,
certifies that he or she is the duly elected Secretary of this corporation and that the above is a true and correct copy of the resolution that was duly adopted at a meeting of the board of directors which was held in accordance with state law and the By-Laws of the corporation on _____ , 19 ___.

I further certify that such resolution is now in full force and effect.

Dated _____

Seal

_____
Secretary of the corporation

Resolution of the Board of Directors of _____ Authorizing Health Care Plan

A meeting of the board of directors of this corporation was duly called and held on _____ , 19 ___.

A quorum of the board of directors was present and at the meeting it was decided, by majority vote, that it is advisable that the corporation provide a health care plan for its employees.

Therefore, it is
RESOLVED, that this corporation adopts and approves the Corporate Health Care Plan dated _____ , 19 ___ , a copy of which is attached to this resolution and which is made a part of the permanent records of this corporation.

The officers of this corporation are authorized to perform all necessary acts to carry out this resolution.

The undersigned, _____ ,
certifies that he or she is the duly elected Secretary of this corporation and that the above is a true and correct copy of the resolution that was duly adopted at a meeting of the board of directors which was held in accordance with state law and the By-Laws of the corporation on _____ , 19 ___.

I further certify that such resolution is now in full force and effect.

Dated _____

Seal

_____
Secretary of the corporation

Resolution of the Board of Directors of _____ Authorizing Group Insurance Plan

A meeting of the board of directors of this corporation was duly called and held on _____ , 19 ___.

A quorum of the board of directors was present and at the meeting it was decided, by majority vote, that it is advisable for the corporation to provide group insurance for its employees.

Therefore, it is
RESOLVED, that this corporation adopts and approves the Corporate Group Insurance Plan dated _____ , 19 ___ , a copy of which is attached to this resolution and which is made a part of the permanent records of this corporation.

The officers of this corporation are authorized to perform all necessary acts to carry out this resolution.

The undersigned, _____ ,
certifies that he or she is the duly elected Secretary of this corporation and that the above is a true and correct copy of the resolution that was duly adopted at a meeting of the board of directors which was held in accordance with state law and the By-Laws of the corporation on _____ , 19 ___.

I further certify that such resolution is now in full force and effect.

Dated _____

Seal

_____
Secretary of the corporation

Resolution of the Board of Directors of _____ Authorizing Death Benefit Plan

A meeting of the board of directors of this corporation was duly called and held on _____ , 19 ___.

A quorum of the board of directors was present and at the meeting it was decided, by majority vote, that it is advisable that the corporation provide a death benefit plan for its employees.

Therefore, it is
RESOLVED, that this corporation adopts and approves the Corporate Death Benefit Plan dated _____ , 19 ___ , a copy of which is attached to this resolution and which is made a part of the permanent records of this corporation.

The officers of this corporation are authorized to perform all necessary acts to carry out this resolution.

The undersigned, _____ , certifies that he or she is the duly elected Secretary of this corporation and that the above is a true and correct copy of the resolution that was duly adopted at a meeting of the board of directors which was held in accordance with state law and the By-Laws of the corporation on _____ , 19 ___.

I further certify that such resolution is now in full force and effect.

Dated _____

Seal

_____
Secretary of the corporation

Resolution of the Board of Directors of _____ Authorizing Employee Benefit Plan

A meeting of the board of directors of this corporation was duly called and held on _____ , 19 ___.

A quorum of the board of directors was present and at the meeting it was decided, by majority vote, that it is advisable that the corporation provide an employee benefit plan for its employees.

Therefore, it is
RESOLVED, that this corporation adopts and approves the Corporate Employee Benefit Plan dated _____ , 19 ___ , a copy of which is attached to this resolution and which is made a part of the permanent records of this corporation.

The officers of this corporation are authorized to perform all necessary acts to carry out this resolution.

The undersigned, _____ , certifies that he or she is the duly elected Secretary of this corporation and that the above is a true and correct copy of the resolution that was duly adopted at a meeting of the board of directors which was held in accordance with state law and the By-Laws of the corporation on _____ , 19 ___.

I further certify that such resolution is now in full force and effect.

Dated _____

Seal

_____
Secretary of the corporation

Resolution of the Board of Directors of _____ Authorizing Rescinding Prior Resolution

A meeting of the board of directors of this corporation was duly called and held on _____ , 19 ___ .

A quorum of the board of directors was present and at the meeting it was decided, by majority vote, that it is in the best interests of the corporation that the resolution of the board of directors dated _____ , 19 ___ , relating to the following matter:

no longer be in effect.

Therefore, it is
RESOLVED, that this corporation rescinds and revokes the resolution of the board of directors dated _____ , 19 ___ , relating to:

The officers of this corporation are hereby authorized to perform all necessary acts to carry out this resolution rescinding and revoking the prior resolution.

The undersigned, _____ , certifies that he or she is the duly elected Secretary of this corporation and that the above is a true and correct copy of the resolution that was duly adopted at a meeting of the board of directors which was held in accordance with state law and the By-Laws of the corporation on _____ , 19 ___ .

I further certify that such resolution is now in full force and effect.

Dated _____

Seal

_____
Secretary of the corporation

Resolution of the Board of Directors of _____ Authorizing Loan to Officer

A meeting of the board of directors of this corporation was duly called and held on _____ , 19 ___ .

A quorum of the board of directors was present and at the meeting it was decided, by majority vote, that _____ , the _____ of this corporation, shall be allowed to borrow $_____ from this corporation.

Therefore, it is
RESOLVED, that this corporation loan $_____ to
_____ , an officer of this corporation on the following terms:

The officers of this corporation are hereby authorized to perform all necessary acts to carry out this resolution.

The undersigned, _____ , certifies that he or she is the duly elected Secretary of this corporation and that the above is a true and correct copy of the resolution that was duly adopted at a meeting of the board of directors which was held in accordance with state law and the By-Laws of the corporation on
_____ , 19 ___ .

I further certify that such resolution is now in full force and effect.

Dated _____

Seal

_____
Secretary of the corporation

Resolution of the Board of Directors of _____ Authorizing Officers Salaries

A meeting of the board of directors of this corporation was duly called and held on _____ , 19 ___.

A quorum of the board of directors was present and at the meeting it was decided, by majority vote, that it is advisable that the annual salary of the _____ of the corporation be $ _____ .

Therefore, it is
RESOLVED, that this corporation provide an annual salary of
$ _____ to the _____ of this corporation.

The officers of this corporation are hereby authorized to perform all necessary acts to carry out this resolution.

The undersigned, _____ , certifies that he or she is the duly elected Secretary of this corporation and that the above is a true and correct copy of the resolution that was duly adopted at a meeting of the board of directors which was held in accordance with state law and the By-Laws of the corporation on _____ , 19 ___.

I further certify that such resolution is now in full force and effect.

Dated _____

Seal

_____
Secretary of the corporation

Resolution of the Board of Directors of _____ Authorizing Stock Transfer

A meeting of the board of directors of this corporation was duly called and held on _____ , 19 ___.

A quorum of the board of directors was present and at the meeting it was decided, by majority vote, that _____ shares of the common stock of the corporation be transferred from

_____ to

_____ .

Therefore, it is
RESOLVED, that this corporation approves the transfer of _____ shares of the common stock of this corporation
from _____ to

_____ .

Such transfer shall be entered into the Stock Transfer Records of this corporation.

The officers of this corporation are hereby authorized to perform all necessary acts to carry out this resolution.

The undersigned, _____ ,
certifies that he or she is the duly elected Secretary of this corporation and that the above is a true and correct copy of the resolution that was duly adopted at a meeting of the board of directors which was held in accordance with state law and the By-Laws of the corporation on _____ , 19 ___.

I further certify that such resolution is now in full force and effect.

Dated _____

Seal

_____
Secretary of the corporation

Resolution of the Board of Directors of _____
Authorizing Change of Registered Office

A meeting of the board of directors of this corporation was duly called and held on _____ , 19 ___.

A quorum of the board of directors was present and at the meeting it was decided, by majority vote, that it is necessary to change the location of the registered office of this corporation from:

to:

Therefore, it is
RESOLVED, that this corporation changes its registered office from the location of:

to:

This address change shall be entered into the corporate records on file with the State of _____. The officers of this corporation are hereby authorized to perform all necessary acts to carry out this resolution.

The undersigned, _____ ,
certifies that he or she is the duly elected Secretary of this corporation and that the above is a true and correct copy of the resolution that was duly adopted at a meeting of the board of directors which was held in accordance with state law and the By-Laws of the corporation on _____ , 19 ___.
I further certify that such resolution is now in full force and effect.

Dated _____

                                                        Seal

_____
Secretary of the corporation

Resolution of the Board of Directors of _____ Authorizing Purchases by President

A meeting of the board of directors of this corporation was duly called and held on _____ , 19 ___.

A quorum of the board of directors was present and at the meeting it was decided, by majority vote, that it is advisable to authorize the President of this corporation to have the authority to make day-to-day purchases for the corporation.

Therefore, it is
RESOLVED, that this corporation authorizes the President of this corporation to make all day-to-day purchases for the benefit of the corporation that the President deems necessary.

The officers of this corporation are hereby authorized to perform all necessary acts to carry out this resolution.

The undersigned, _____ , certifies that he or she is the duly elected Secretary of this corporation and that the above is a true and correct copy of the resolution that was duly adopted at a meeting of the board of directors which was held in accordance with state law and the By-Laws of the corporation on _____ , 19 ___.

I further certify that such resolution is now in full force and effect.

Dated _____

Seal

_____
Secretary of the corporation

Resolution of the Board of Directors of _____ Authorizing Bonus

A meeting of the board of directors of this corporation was duly called and held on _____ , 19 ___.

A quorum of the board of directors was present and at the meeting it was decided, by majority vote, that it is advisable to provide a bonus to the following employee of this corporation:

Therefore, it is
RESOLVED, that this corporation pay a bonus in the amount of
$_____ to _____ ,
an employee of the corporation.

The officers of this corporation are hereby authorized to perform all necessary acts to carry out this resolution.

The undersigned, _____ ,
certifies that he or she is the duly elected Secretary of this corporation and that the above is a true and correct copy of the resolution that was duly adopted at a meeting of the board of directors which was held in accordance with state law and the By-Laws of the corporation on
_____ , 19 ___.

I further certify that such resolution is now in full force and effect.

Dated _____

                                                      Seal

_____
Secretary of the corporation

Resolution of the Shareholders of _____
Authorizing the Sale of All Corporate Assets

A meeting of the shareholders of this corporation was duly called and held on _____ , 19 ___.

A quorum of the shareholders was present, in person or by proxy, and at the meeting it was decided, by majority vote, that it is in the best interests of the corporation that all of the corporate assets, consisting of those items listed on the List of Corporate Assets which is attached to this resolution, be sold to _____ of

_____.

Therefore, it is
RESOLVED, that this corporation sell all of the corporate assets listed on the List of Corporate Assets which is attached to this resolution, be sold to _____ of _____

_____.

The officers of this corporation are hereby authorized to perform all necessary acts to carry out this resolution.

The undersigned, _____ ,
certifies that he or she is the duly elected Secretary of this corporation and that the above is a true and correct copy of the resolution that was duly adopted at a meeting of the shareholders which was held in accordance with state law and the By-Laws of the corporation on _____ , 19 ___.

I further certify that such resolution is now in full force and effect.

Dated _____

Seal

_____
Secretary of the corporation

Consent Resolutions

Any of the resolution forms which are contained in this chapter can easily be adapted for use as consent resolutions. First, however, it must be verified that the By-Laws of the corporation allow the use of consent resolutions for directors and shareholders. The By-Laws which are presented in this book contain the following clauses which allow consent resolutions to be used:

> For shareholders: "Any action which may be taken at a shareholders meeting may be taken instead without a meeting if a resolution is consented to, in writing, by all shareholders who would be entitled to vote on the matter."

> For directors: "Any action which may be taken at a directors meeting may be taken instead without a meeting if a resolution is consented to, in writing, by all directors."

If you are operating under different By-Laws, be certain that your By-laws contains a substantially similar authorization for consent resolutions.

The use of consent resolutions allows for a much greater flexibility in the management of corporations. Formal meetings are not necessary, although for many issues, meetings may be highly recommended as a method to record the remarks and positions of board members or shareholders who may oppose the action. Consent resolutions are most useful in those situations where the board of directors or number of shareholders is small and all of the directors or shareholders are in complete agreement regarding the action to be taken.

In order to adapt the standard resolutions in this and other chapters of this book for use as consent resolutions, simply alter the form in the following three ways (substitute *shareholders* where appropriate if you are preparing a shareholders consent resolution):

> 1.   Add the word "Consent" to the title (For example: Consent Resolution of the Board of Directors of the ABCXYZ Corporation).

> 2. Substitute the following for the first paragraph of the resolution:

> > The undersigned, being all of the directors (or shareholders) of this corporation and acting in accordance with state law and the By-Laws of this corporation, consent to the adoption of the following as if it was adopted at a duly called

meeting of the board of directors (or shareholders) of this corporation. By unanimous consent of the board of directors (or shareholders) of this corporation, it is decided that:

3. Add signature lines for all of the directors (or shareholders) of the corporation. After all of the signatures, insert the following phrase:

Being all of the directors (or shareholders) of the corporation.

4. Substitute the following for the last paragraph of the resolution:

The undersigned, _____, certifies that he or she is the duly elected Secretary of this corporation and that the above is a true and correct copy of the resolution that was duly adopted by consent of the board of directors (or shareholders) in accordance with state law and the By-Laws of the corporation on _____, 19 ___. I further certify that such resolution is now in full force and effect.

On the following page, you will find a General Directors Consent Resolution which has been adapted with these instructions from the General Directors Resolution form which was shown on page 143.

Consent Resolution of the Board of Directors
of _____

The undersigned, being all of the directors of this corporation and acting in accordance with state law and the By-Laws of this corporation, consent to the adoption of the following as if it was adopted at a duly called meeting of the board of directors of this corporation. By unanimous consent of the board of directors of this corporation, it is decided that

Therefore, it is
RESOLVED, that this corporation:

The officers of this corporation are hereby authorized to perform all necessary acts to carry out this resolution.

Dated _____

_____   _____
Director of the corporation   Director of the corporation

_____   _____
Director of the corporation   Director of the corporation

Being all of the Directors of this corporation.

The undersigned, _____ ,
certifies that he or she is the duly elected Secretary of this corporation and that the above is a true and correct copy of the resolution that was duly adopted by consent of the board of directors in accordance with state law and the By-Laws of the corporation on _____ ,
19 ___.

I further certify that such resolution is now in full force and effect.

Dated _____

                                                    Seal

_____
Secretary of the corporation

Chapter 11

Corporate Stock

Corporate stock represents the money or property which is invested in a corporation. It is a representation of the share of ownership in a corporate business. When a corporation files its Articles of Incorporation with the state, it states how many shares of stock it will be authorized to issue (For example: 500 shares). When the authorized shares are sold or transferred to a shareholder for something of value (money, property, or labor), the shares are said to be "issued and outstanding". All of the authorized shares need not be issued. The ownership of the shares in the corporation is then evidenced by a stock certificate describing the number of shares owned. The value of the shares can be a specific "par" value (for example: $1.00 per share) or they can be "no par" value, which allows the board of directors to fix the value of the shares by resolution. If the shares are given a par value, the stock must be sold for at least the stated par value. The concept of par value is gradually being eliminated from modern business corporation acts, allowing board of director discretion to fix the value of the shares. All states allow the use of no-par stock.

An example may best illustrate the use of stock. A corporation is formed and 500 shares of no-par value common stock are authorized in the Articles of Incorporation. 3 people will form the initial shareholders of the corporation, with one desiring to own 50% of the shares and the other two desiring to own 25% each. All three comprise the board of directors. As a board, they decide to issue 300 shares of stock and they decide to fix the value per share at $10.00. Thus, the majority owner will pay the corporation $1,500.00 ($10.00 X 150 shares or 50% of the issued and outstanding shares—*not* 50% of the authorized shares). The other two shareholders will pay $750.00 each for 75 shares apiece of the issued shares. The ownership of the shares which have been issued will be represented by stock certificates which will be delivered to each of the owners. The transactions will be recorded in the corporation's stock transfer book. At the close of these transactions, the corporation will have 3 shareholders: one with 150 shares of issued and outstanding stock and two with 75 shares of issued and outstanding stock. The corporation will have $3,000.00 of paid-in capital. 200 shares will remain as authorized but not issued or outstanding. At shareholder meetings, each share of issued and outstanding stock will represent one vote. (See Chapter 8).

The above scenario presents stock ownership at its most basic. The shares described were no-par value common stock. There are many, many variable characteristics which can be given to stock. The forms in this book are based on basic single-class common stock with voting rights. Classes of stock may, however, be created with non-voting attributes, with preferences for dividends, and with many other different characteristics. Most small business corporations can operate efficiently with a single class of common stock with voting rights. There is no requirement that the stock certificate be in a particular format. The stock certificates for use in this book are a simple generic form. If you desire, you may obtain fancy blank stock certificates from most office supply stores, but these are not required. For the issuance of stock, follow the steps shown below in the Stock Checklist. Each of the steps taken at a meeting of the board of directors must be documented with a board resolution (see Chapter 9).

Stock Checklist

❑ Designate the number of authorized shares in Articles of Incorporation and whether they are par or no-par value.

❑ At the initial board of directors meeting, determine the number of shares to be issued.

❑ If the shares are no-par, at the initial board of directors meeting, determine the value of the shares.

❑ At a board of directors meeting, determine who will purchase shares and how many will be sold to each person.

❑ If necessary, at a board of directors meeting, the board of directors must fix the value of any property which will be accepted in exchange for shares of stock.

❑ At a board of directors meeting, authorize officers to issue shares to persons designated.

❑ The Secretary will then prepare the appropriate stock certificates.

❑ If there are restrictions on the transfer of stock, note the restrictions on the back of the certificate. (See Chapter 12).

❑ All of the officers of the corporation will sign the certificates.

❑ The Secretary will receive the money or property from the purchasers and deposit any funds in the corporate bank account.

❑ The Secretary will issue the certificates and receipts for money or property and record the transaction in the corporate stock transfer book.

❑ If a certificate is lost, use the Lost Stock Affidavit at the end of the chapter.

Corporate Stock Certificate (Generic-Front)

Certificate Number: _____

Number of Shares: _____

Corporate Stock Certificate

Name of Corporation _____

A business corporation incorporated under the laws of the State of: _____
Par Value of Shares: $ _____ **Number of Shares Authorized:** _____

This Certifies That

_____ is the owner of _____ shares

of common stock of this corporation. The shares represented are fully paid and are non-assessable. The shares represented by this Certificate are only transferable on the official books of the Corporation by the holder of this Certificate, in person or by Attorney. For transfer, this Certificate must be properly endorsed on the back and surrendered to the Corporation. This Certificate is signed by all of the Officers of this Corporation.

Dated _____

President _____   Vice-President _____

Secretary _____   Treasurer _____

Corporate Stock Certificate (Generic-Back)

For value received, I, _____, the owner of this Certificate, transfer the number of shares represented by this Certificate to _____, and I instruct the Secretary of this Corporation to record this transfer on the books of the Corporation. Any restrictions on the transfer of these shares are shown below.

Dated _____

Signature _____

Restrictions on Transfer:

Stock Transfer Book

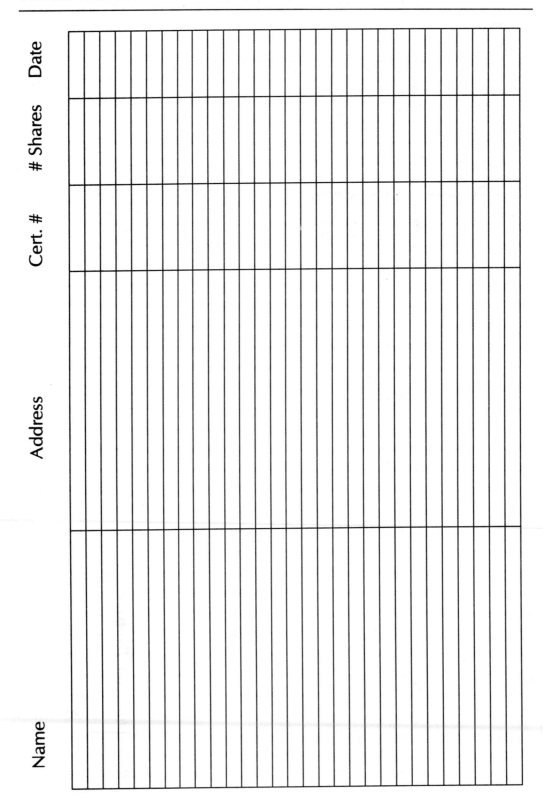

Receipt for Stock Certificate of _____

On this date, _____ , a
shareholder in this corporation has purchased _____
shares of common stock in this corporation, represented by Stock
Certificate number _____.

This Certificate represents _____ percent of ownership
in this corporation.

The shareholder has transferred to the corporation the following assets,
with a fair market value of $ _____ in consideration for
the receipt of the shares of stock:

Payment in full has been received for these shares and the shares have
been issued by the corporation, transferred to the shareholder, and
received by the shareholder.

Record of this transaction has been recorded in the Stock Transfer Book of
this corporation.

Date _____

_____
Secretary of the corporation

_____
Shareholder

Lost Stock Affidavit

State of _____)
)   S.S.
County of _____)

Being duly sworn, the undersigned states the following on oath:

1. My name is _____ and my
   addresss is _____ , City of
   _____ , State of _____ .

2. I am the lawful owner of _____ shares of issued
   and outstanding common stock of _____ ,
   a corporation registered in the State of _____ .

3. I have not sold, exchanged, transferred or pledged any of these
   shares in any manner and the shares have been in my sole
   possession at my residence since issuance. I am now unable to
   locate these shares and believe that they have been lost, stolen, or
   misplaced.

4. I request the issuing corporation to issue a duplicate stock certificate
   for ownership of these shares without surrender of the original
   shares.

5. I agree to indemnify and hold the issuing corporation harmless from
   any liability or expenses which may result from reliance on this
   affidavit.

_____ _____
Signature   Date

Subscribed and sworn to before me on _____ , 19 ___ .

_____
Notary Public, in and for the County of _____ , State of
_____ . My commission expires _____ .

Chapter 12

Corporate Shareholder Agreement

For many smaller corporations with only a few shareholders, some form of shareholder agreement is often useful. Although shareholder agreements can take many forms, the most common specify certain restrictions on the ability to sell shares of the corporations stock to outside investors. Restrictions on the ability to transfer shares allow the corporation to have greater control regarding who is a shareholder, and, thus, ultimately who is allowed to select the board of directors of the corporation.

The agreement which is contained in this chapter addresses several of the major concerns regarding stock transfers. First, the agreement restricts the rights of shareholders to transfer their stock except by the terms of the agreement. Second, it provides a "right of first refusal" to both the corporation and to the other shareholders on any proposed sale of stock. The agreement also provides for a buy-out/sell-out restriction. This particular restriction requires that if a shareholder desires to buy all of the shares of the corporation, she/he must be willing to also sell all of her/his shares on the same terms. Thus, if a shareholder desires to have total control, it becomes an all-or-nothing proposition. If the other shareholders agree, the deal will go through. But if the other shareholders desire to retain control, the one who proposed the buy-out must sell out to the remaining shareholders. Finally, the agreement provides for methods for determining the value of the shares for sales upon death or resignation.

Shareholders Stock Purchase Agreement of _____

This Agreement is made on _____ , 19 ___ between
_____ , a corporation
incorporated under the laws of the State of _____ and
the following shareholders of this corporation

_____
_____
_____
_____ .

The shareholders listed above own all of the issued and outstanding stock of this corporation. The corporation and its shareholders desire to provide for continuity in the ownership and management of this corporation.

THEREFORE, in consideration of the mutual promises in this Agreement, and for other good and valuable consideration, the parties agree as follows:

1. **Restrictions**. No shareholder shall transfer, mortgage, encumber or dispose of any or all of their shares except as allowed in this Agreement.

2. **Transfer Outside The Corporation**. If a shareholder wishes to dispose of any shares, other than to the corporation, 30 days written notice must be given to the corporation. This notice must state the number of shares to be transferred, the name and address of the person or company to whom the transfer is proposed, the purchase price amount, and the date of the proposed transfer.

    The corporation will have 30 days after receipt of the written notice to exercise an option to buy any or all of the shares on the same terms as the proposed transfer.

    If the corporation does not exercise its option, then within its 30-day option period, the corporation must provide written notice to all of the other shareholders of the corporation. Then any or all of the other shareholders of the corporation will have an additional 30 days to exercise an option to buy any or all of the shares on the same terms as the proposed transfer. Each shareholder will have an option to buy a percentage of the proposed transfer amount equal to the number of shares owned by that shareholder divided by the total number of shares issued and outstanding, not including the number of shares which are included in the proposed transfer. If a shareholder does not exercise its option to buy, then the percentage will be determined without including that shareholder's shares in the total shares outstanding.

Acting separately or together, the corporation and the shareholders must agree to purchase all of the shares offered in the proposed transfer. If neither the corporation nor the shareholders elect to buy all of the shares offered in the proposed transfer, then 60 days after the corporation's receipt of the written notice of the proposed transfer, the shareholder may sell the shares as stated in the written notice of proposed transfer.

3. ***Offer To Buy or Sell All Shares.*** If a shareholder wishes to sell all of her/his shares or buy all of the shares of all the other shareholders in the corporation, the shareholder must provide written notice that she/he is willing to either sell all of his/her shares or buy all of the outstanding shares of other shareholders. The shareholder must be willing to allow either event to happen.

Within 30 days of receipt of the written notice, any or all of the other shareholders of the corporation will have an option to buy any or all of the shares on the same terms as the proposed transaction. Each shareholder will have an option to buy a percentage of the shares of the shareholder requesting the buy/sell transaction. The percentage will be the number of shares owned by that shareholder divided by the number of shares issued and outstanding, not including the number of shares which are owned by the shareholder proposing the transaction. If a shareholder does not exercise its option to buy, then the percentage will be determined without including that shareholder's shares in the total shares outstanding and the remaining shareholders will have an additional 30 days in which to exercise their own options.

Acting separately or together, the other shareholders must either agree to purchase all of the shares owned by the shareholder proposing the buy/sell transaction or allow all of their own shares to be purchased. If the shareholders do not elect to buy all of the shares offered in the proposed transfer, then 60 days after the receipt of the written notice of the proposed transaction, the shareholder proposing the transaction shall be obligated to purchase all of the shares of the other shareholders as stated in the written notice of proposed transaction and that all the other shareholders will be obligated to sell all of their shares.

4. ***Involuntary Transfer of Shares.*** If a shareholder's shares are transferred by operation of law, other than by death, the corporation and other shareholders shall have 60 days to exercise an option to purchase all of such shares under the option terms of Paragraph #2 of this Agreement. If a price is paid upon the involuntary transfer, then this will be the price for the exercise of the option. If no price is paid, the price will be determined as specified under Paragraph #8 of this Agreement.

5. ***Death of a Shareholder.*** On the death of a shareholder, the corporation will purchase all of the deceased shareholder's shares at the price as specified in Paragraph #8 of this Agreement. The deceased shareholder's estate must sell the shares to the corporation.

6. ***Disability of Shareholder.*** If any shareholder shall suffer a permanent disability which prevents him/her from performing his/her usual duties for 1 year, the corporation may elect to purchase all of the shareholders shares. Written notice must be provided to the shareholder or his/her representatives within 30 days after the 1 year period. The purchase price will be as specified in Paragraph #8 of this Agreement. The disabled shareholder or his/her representatives must sell the shares to the corporation.

7. ***Resignation or Discharge of a Shareholder.*** If any shareholder voluntarily resigns from employment with the corporation, or is discharged from employment with the corporation for reasonable cause, then the corporation will buy all of the shareholder's shares at a purchase price as specified under Paragraph #8 of this Agreement. The shareholder must sell the shares to the corporation.

8. ***Purchase Price of Shares.*** For purchases under Paragraph #2, the purchase price will be as provided by Paragraph #2. For all other purchases, the purchase price will be as follows:
    For shares to be sold prior to _____, 19 ___ , the purchase price will be $ _____ . The shareholders agree to redetermine the purchase price prior to _____ , 19 ___ .
    For each succeeding year, the shareholders agree to redetermine the purchase price at a special meeting which will take place within 60 days prior to the end of the corporation's fiscal year. The valuation

will be in the form of a Shareholder's Resolution and be signed by all shareholders.

If the shareholders fail to make any of the required redeterminations of purchase price, then the purchase price will be determined by the Certified Public Accountant for the corporation as of the last day of the month preceding the proposed transaction. The method for valuation will be as follows:

9.   **Closing of Transactions.** The closing of any transaction under this Agreement will take place at the offices of the corporation. The Closing Date will be determined under the appropriate paragraph or if not provided, then 90 days after the first notice of the proposed transaction. Upon closing, the buyer will deliver to the seller at least 50% of the purchase price in cash, with the other 50% in the form of a promissory note bearing 10% annual interest payable within 3 years, with payments amortized and payable on the first of each month following the closing date. The note may be prepaid without penalty and will provide that if any payment is not made by the due date, the entire note is immediately due and payable. Upon receipt of the required cash and/or promissory note, the seller shall deliver the appropriate shares to the buyer.

10.   **Certificate Endorsement**. All shares issued by the corporation will bear the following endorsement:
> The ownership and transfer of the shares of stock evidenced by this Certificate are specifically restricted by the provisions of a Shareholders Stock Purchase Agreement executed by the shareholder whose name appears on the face of this Certificate and by the corporation and all remaining shareholders of the corporation. The Agreement restricts all sales or purchases of shares of stock of this corporation and provides various purchase options.

11.   **Termination.** This Agreement will terminate:

a. On _____ , 19 ___; or
b. By unanimous agreement of all shareholders; or
c. On the death of all shareholders; or
d. On the corporation's filing for voluntary bankruptcy.

12. **Additional Provisions.**

13. **Miscellaneous Provisions.** This Agreement is binding on the corporation, the shareholders, their heirs, legal representatives, successors, or assigns. This Agreement will be governed by the laws of the State of _____ . This Agreement may be amended only by unanimous written consent of the corporation and all of its shareholders.

Dated _____

_____
Name of corporation

By:

_____
The President of the corporation

                                            Seal

_____   _____
Shareholder   Shareholder

_____   _____
Shareholder   Shareholder

_____   _____
Shareholder   Shareholder

_____   _____
Shareholder   Shareholder

Being all of the shareholders of this corporation.

Chapter 13

"S" Corporation Status

An "S" corporation is a type of corporation which is recognized by the U.S. Internal Revenue Service and is treated differently than other corporations in terms of federal taxation. Some states also recognize "S" corporation status for state income taxation purposes; some states do not. The only reason for becoming an "S" corporation is to obtain a different method of taxation than other corporations.

For standard corporations, the corporation pays a federal and, perhaps, state corporate tax on the business profits. If the after-tax profit is then distributed to the shareholders as dividends, the shareholders then pay an additional personal income tax on the dividends. The amount distributed to the shareholders as dividends is not a deduction for the corporation. "S" corporations, on the other hand, are taxed similarly to partnerships. They act merely as a conduit for passing the income and deductions of the corporation directly through to the individual shareholders in much the same manner as partnerships, or even sole proprietorships. The "S" corporation does not pay a corporate tax and files a different type of tax form than does a standard corporation. (See Chapter 14). Taxation of the profits of the "S" corporation falls to the individuals who own shares in the corporation. This also allows for each individual shareholder to personally deduct their share of any corporate losses.

There are, however, certain basic requirements for qualifying a corporation for "S" corporation status. Every requirement must be met before the IRS will recognize "S" corporation status and allow for the different tax treatment.

① The corporation must have no more than 35 shareholders. (Wives and husbands, even if they own stock separately, are considered as only one shareholder.)

② Each of the corporation's shareholders must be a natural person or the estate of a natural person. Corporations and partnerships may not hold shares in the corporation. Each shareholder must also be a citizen or resident of the United States.

③ The corporation must only have one class of stock which is issued and outstanding. The corporation may have other classes of stock which are authorized, providing no shares are issued. Different voting rights within a class of stock (ie. voting and non-voting) do not disqualify the corporation.

④ The corporation must already be incorporated in one of the United States or its possessions. Financial institutions, foreign corporations, and certain other very specialized corporations are not eligible.

⑤ The corporation must not have been qualified as an "S" corporation within the previous 5 years. This restrictions prevents abrupt shifting from one type of corporation to another in order to obtain the maximum tax benefits.

⑥ The corporation must file *Form 2553*: **Election by a Small Business Corporation** with the IRS.

If your corporation meets all of these requirements, "S" corporation status may be elected. It may be prudent to obtain the advice of a competent accountant prior to making the election, however. The actual steps in electing "S" corporation status are detailed below in the "S" Corporation Checklist. Following the Checklist are the forms required to complete the election of "S" corporation status. Please note that *IRS Form 2553*: **Election by a Small Business Corporation** is only provided for illustration purposes and a copy of the form should be obtained from the IRS.

"S" Corporation Checklist

❑ Determine that the corporation has fewer than 35 shareholders.

❑ Determine that all shareholders are natural persons or estates.

❑ Determine that the corporation has only one class of stock issued and outstanding.

❑ Determine that the corporation is already incorporated in the U.S or one of its possessions.

❑ Determine that the corporation has not had "S" status within the past 5 years.

❑ All shareholders must consent to the election to be treated as an "S" corporation.

❑ Notice of a special shareholders meeting for the purpose of consenting to the election as an "S" corporation should be provided to all shareholders of record.

❑ A special shareholders meeting should be held at which all shareholders of the corporation consent to the election by the corporation to be treated as an "S" corporation.

❑ A shareholders resolution consenting to the election to be treated as an "S" corporation should be signed by all shareholders of record.

❑ The Secretary of the corporation should complete *IRS Form 2553*: ***Election by a Small Business Corporation***.

❑ All shareholders of record must sign *IRS Form 2553*: ***Election by a Small Business Corporation***.

❑ The secretary of the corporation should file *IRS Form 2553*: ***Election by a Small Business Corporation***.

Notice of Special Shareholders Meeting of _____ Regarding "S" Corporation Status

TO:

In accordance with the By-Laws of this corporation, an official special meeting of the shareholders will be held at _____ m., on _____ , 19 ___ , at the offices of the corporation located at _____.

The purpose of this meeting is to discuss the election of "S" corporation status for the corporation, under Internal Revenue Code Section 1362.

The Stock Transfer Book of this corporation will remain closed from _____ , 19 ___ until _____ , 19 ___.

Dated _____

                                                        Seal

_____
Secretary of the corporation

Affidavit of Mailing of Notice of Special Shareholders Meeting of _____ Regarding "S" Corporation Status

State of _____   )
)   S.S.
County of _____   )

Being duly sworn, _____ states:

I am the Secretary of _____ , a
corporation organized under the laws of the State of _____ .

On _____ , 19 ___ , I personally deposited stamped and
sealed copies of Notice of the Special Shareholders Meeting of this
corporation in a post-office box in the City of _____ , in
the State of _____ .

The copies were correctly addressed to all shareholders of this
corporation as of _____ , 19 ___ as shown in the Stock
Transfer Book of this corporation. The list of names and addresses of the
shareholders is attached to this Affidavit.

_____
Secretary of the corporation

Subscribed and Sworn to before me on _____ , 19 ___ .

_____
Notary Public in and for the County of _____ and the
State of _____ . My commission expires
_____ .

Waiver of Notice of Special Shareholders Meeting of _____ Regarding "S" Corporation Status

We, the undersigned shareholders of this corporation, waive any required notice and consent to the holding of the special meeting of the shareholders of this corporation on _____ , 19 ___ , at _____ m., at the offices of the corporation, located at
_____
_____ .

Dated _____

Name   Signature

_____   _____

_____   _____

_____   _____

_____   _____

_____   _____

_____   _____

_____   _____

_____   _____

Minutes of Special Shareholders Meeting of _____ Regarding "S" Corporation Status

A special meeting of the shareholders of this corporation was held on _____ , 19 ___ , at _____ m., at the offices of the corporation located at _____ _____ .

The President of this corporation, _____ ,
and the Vice-President of this corporation, _____ ,
and the Secretary of this corporation, _____ ,
and the Treasurer of this corporation, _____ ,
were present. Other than shareholders, the following other persons were also present:

_____
_____ .

1. The President of this corporation called the meeting to order and determined that a quorum was present, either in person or by proxy.

    The following shareholders were present in person:

    Name   Number of Shares

    _____   _____

    _____   _____

    _____   _____

    _____   _____

    _____   _____

    _____   _____

    _____   _____

The following shareholders were represented by proxy:

Name   Number of Shares

_____   _____

_____   _____

_____   _____

2. The Secretary of this corporation reported that notice of the meeting had been properly given or waived by each shareholder in accordance with the By-Laws. Upon motion made and carried, the Secretary was directed to attach the appropriate Notice and Affidavit or Waiver to these minutes.

3. _____ was then elected Chairperson of this meeting.

4. The following business was discussed: The benefits and advantages of the shareholders electing to obtain "S" corporation status under Internal Revenue Code Section 1362.

5. Upon motion made and carried, the following resolution was approved unanimously by outstanding shares of this corporation: RESOLVED that:
    This corporation elects to be treated and taxed as an "S" corporation under Internal Revenue Section 1362.

6. The President declared that this shareholders resolution was duly adopted.

There being no further business, upon motion made and carried the meeting was adjourned.

Dated _____

                                            Seal

_____
Secretary of the corporation

Resolution of the Shareholders of _____ Regarding "S" Corporation Status

A special meeting of the shareholders of this corporation was duly called and held on _____ , 19 ___. All of the shareholders of this corporation were present, in person or by proxy.

At the meeting it was decided, by unanimous vote, that it is in the best interests of the corporation that the corporation elect to be treated as an "S" corporation under the provisions of Internal Revenue Code Section 1362.

Therefore, it is unanimously

RESOLVED, that this corporation elects to be treated as an "S" corporation under the provisions of Internal Revenue Code Section 1362. The officers of this corporation are hereby authorized to perform all necessary acts to carry out this resolution.

The undersigned, _____ , certifies that he or she is the duly elected Secretary of this corporation and that the above is a true and correct copy of the resolution that was duly adopted at a meeting of the shareholders which was held in accordance with state law and the By-Laws of the corporation on _____ , 19 ___. I further certify that such resolution is now in full force and effect.

Dated _____

Seal

_____
Secretary of the corporation

Shareholder

Shareholder

Shareholder

Shareholder

Shareholder

Shareholder

Shareholder

Shareholder

Shareholder

Being all of the shareholders of this corporation.

Sample IRS Form 2553:
Election by a Small Business Corporation

Form **2553** (Rev. September 1993) Department of the Treasury Internal Revenue Service	**Election by a Small Business Corporation** (Under section 1362 of the Internal Revenue Code) ▶ For Paperwork Reduction Act Notice, see page 1 of instructions. ▶ See separate instructions.	OMB No. 1545-0146 Expires 8-31-96

Notes: 1. *This election, to be an "S corporation," can be accepted only if all the tests are met under* **Who May Elect** *on page 1 of the instructions; all signatures in Parts I and III are originals (no photocopies); and the exact name and address of the corporation and other required form information are provided.*

2. *Do not file* **Form 1120S**, *U.S. Income Tax Return for an S Corporation, until you are notified that your election is accepted.*

Part I	**Election Information**		

Please Type or Print

Name of corporation (see instructions)	**A** Employer identification number (EIN)
Number, street, and room or suite no. (If a P.O. box, see instructions.)	**B** Date incorporated
City or town, state, and ZIP code	**C** State of incorporation

D Election is to be effective for tax year beginning (month, day, year) . . . . ▶ /   /

E Name and title of officer or legal representative who the IRS may call for more information

F Telephone number of officer or legal representative (   )

G If the corporation changed its name or address after applying for the EIN shown in **A**, check this box . . . . ▶ ☐

H If this election takes effect for the first tax year the corporation exists, enter month, day, and year of the **earliest** of the following: (1) date the corporation first had shareholders, (2) date the corporation first had assets, or (3) date the corporation began doing business . . . . ▶ /   /

I Selected tax year: Annual return will be filed for tax year ending (month and day) ▶ ....

If the tax year ends on any date other than December 31, except for an automatic 52-53-week tax year ending with reference to the month of December, you **must** complete Part II on the back. If the date you enter is the ending date of an automatic 52-53-week tax year, write "52-53-week year" to the right of the date. See Temporary Regulations section 1.441-2T(e)(3).

J Name and address of each shareholder, shareholder's spouse having a community property interest in the corporation's stock, and each tenant in common, joint tenant, and tenant by the entirety. (A husband and wife (and their estates) are counted as one shareholder in determining the number of shareholders without regard to the manner in which the stock is owned.)	**K** Shareholders' Consent Statement. Under penalties of perjury, we declare that we consent to the election of the above-named corporation to be an "S corporation" under section 1362(a) and that we have examined this consent statement, including accompanying schedules and statements, and to the best of our knowledge and belief, it is true, correct, and complete. (Shareholders sign and date below.)*		**L** Stock owned		**M** Social security number or employer identification number (see instructions)	**N** Share-holder's tax year ends (month and day)
	Signature	Date	Number of shares	Dates acquired		

*For this election to be valid, the consent of each shareholder, shareholder's spouse having a community property interest in the corporation's stock, and each tenant in common, joint tenant, and tenant by the entirety must either appear above or be attached to this form. (See instructions for Column K if a continuation sheet or a separate consent statement is needed.)

Under penalties of perjury, I declare that I have examined this election, including accompanying schedules and statements, and to the best of my knowledge and belief, it is true, correct, and complete.

Signature of officer ▶   Title ▶   Date ▶

See Parts II and III on back.   Cat. No. 18629R   Form **2553** (Rev. 9-93)

Form 2553 (Rev. 9-93)

Part II Selection of Fiscal Tax Year (All corporations using this part must complete item O and one of items P, Q, or R.)

O Check the applicable box below to indicate whether the corporation is:

1. ☐ A new corporation adopting the tax year entered in item I, Part I.
2. ☐ An existing corporation retaining the tax year entered in item I, Part I.
3. ☐ An existing corporation changing to the tax year entered in item I, Part I.

P Complete item P if the corporation is using the expeditious approval provisions of Revenue Procedure 87-32, 1987-2 C.B. 396, to request: **(1)** a natural business year (as defined in section 4.01(1) of Rev. Proc. 87-32), or **(2)** a year that satisfies the ownership tax year test in section 4.01(2) of Rev. Proc. 87-32. Check the applicable box below to indicate the representation statement the corporation is making as required under section 4 of Rev. Proc. 87-32.

1. Natural Business Year ► ☐ I represent that the corporation is retaining or changing to a tax year that coincides with its natural business year as defined in section 4.01(1) of Rev. Proc. 87-32 and as verified by its satisfaction of the requirements of section 4.02(1) of Rev. Proc. 87-32. In addition, if the corporation is changing to a natural business year as defined in section 4.01(1), I further represent that such tax year results in less deferral of income to the owners than the corporation's present tax year. I also represent that the corporation is not described in section 3.01(2) of Rev. Proc. 87-32. (See instructions for additional information that must be attached.)

2. Ownership Tax Year ► ☐ I represent that shareholders holding more than half of the shares of the stock (as of the first day of the tax year to which the request relates) of the corporation have the same tax year or are concurrently changing to the tax year that the corporation adopts, retains, or changes to per item I, Part I. I also represent that the corporation is not described in section 3.01(2) of Rev. Proc. 87-32.

Note: *If you do not use item P and the corporation wants a fiscal tax year, complete either item Q or R below. Item Q is used to request a fiscal tax year based on a business purpose and to make a back-up section 444 election. Item R is used to make a regular section 444 election.*

Q Business Purpose—To request a fiscal tax year based on a business purpose, you must check box Q1 and pay a user fee. See instructions for details. You may also check box Q2 and/or box Q3.

1. Check here ► ☐ if the fiscal year entered in item I, Part I, is requested under the provisions of section 6.03 of Rev. Proc. 87-32. Attach to Form 2553 a statement showing the business purpose for the requested fiscal year. See instructions for additional information that must be attached.

2. Check here ► ☐ to show that the corporation intends to make a back-up section 444 election in the event the corporation's business purpose request is not approved by the IRS. (See instructions for more information.)

3. Check here ► ☐ to show that the corporation agrees to adopt or change to a tax year ending December 31 if necessary for the IRS to accept this election for S corporation status in the event: (1) the corporation's business purpose request is not approved and the corporation makes a back-up section 444 election, but is ultimately not qualified to make a section 444 election, or (2) the corporation's business purpose request is not approved and the corporation did not make a back-up section 444 election.

R Section 444 Election—To make a section 444 election, you must check box R1 and you may also check box R2.

1. Check here ► ☐ to show the corporation will make, if qualified, a section 444 election to have the fiscal tax year shown in item I, Part I. To make the election, you must complete **Form 8716**, Election To Have a Tax Year Other Than a Required Tax Year, and either attach it to Form 2553 or file it separately.

2. Check here ► ☐ to show that the corporation agrees to adopt or change to a tax year ending December 31 if necessary for the IRS to accept this election for S corporation status in the event the corporation is ultimately not qualified to make a section 444 election.

Part III Qualified Subchapter S Trust (QSST) Election Under Section 1361(d)(2)**

Income beneficiary's name and address	Social security number
Trust's name and address	Employer identification number

Date on which stock of the corporation was transferred to the trust (month, day, year) . . . . ► / /

In order for the trust named above to be a QSST and thus a qualifying shareholder of the S corporation for which this Form 2553 is filed, I hereby make the election under section 1361(d)(2). Under penalties of perjury, I certify that the trust meets the definitional requirements of section 1361(d)(3) and that all other information provided in Part III is true, correct, and complete.

_____   _____
Signature of income beneficiary or signature and title of legal representative or other qualified person making the election   Date

**Use of Part III to make the QSST election may be made only if stock of the corporation has been transferred to the trust on or before the date on which the corporation makes its election to be an S corporation. The QSST election must be made and filed separately if stock of the corporation is transferred to the trust after the date on which the corporation makes the S election.

♻ Printed on recycled paper   *U.S. Government Printing Office: 1993 — 301-828/80271

Chapter 14

Taxation of Corporations

Corporations are a separate entity under the law and as such are subject to taxation at both the state and federal levels. In general, standard non-"S" corporations are subject to federal income tax on the annual profits in many ways similar to the tax on individual income. However, there are significant differences. The most important aspect is the "double" taxation on corporate income if it is distributed to the shareholders in the form of dividends. At the corporate level, corporate net income is subject to tax at the corporate level. Corporate funds which are distributed to officers or directors in the forms of salaries, expense reimbursements, or employee benefits may be used by a corporation as a legitimate business deduction against the income of the corporation. Corporate surplus funds, however, that are paid out to shareholders in the form of dividends on their ownership of stock in the corporation are not allowed to be used as a corporate deduction. Thus, any funds used in this manner have been subject to corporate income tax prior to distribution to the shareholders. The dividends are then also subject to taxation as income to the shareholder and so are subject to a "double" taxation. "S" corporations are taxed similarly to partnerships, with the corporation acting only as a conduit and all of the deductions and income passing to the individual shareholders where they are subject to income tax. Corporations, however, may be used by businesses in many ways to actually lessen the federal and state income tax burdens. A competent tax professional should be consulted. The federal tax forms which are contained in this chapter are for illustrative purposes only. A brief study of them will provide you with an overview of the method by which corporations are taxed.

Form 1120

Department of the Treasury
Internal Revenue Service

U.S. Corporation Income Tax Return

For calendar year 1993 or tax year beginning .... , 1993, ending .... , 19 ...
▶ Instructions are separate. See page 1 for Paperwork Reduction Act Notice.

OMB No. 1545-0123

1993

A Check if a:
1 Consolidated return (attach Form 851) ☐
2 Personal holding co. (attach Sch. PH) ☐
3 Personal service corp. (as defined in Temporary Regs. sec. 1.441-4T— see instructions) ☐

Use IRS label. Otherwise, please print or type.

Name

Number, street, and room or suite no. (If a P.O. box, see page 7 of instructions.)

City or town, state, and ZIP code

B Employer identification number

C Date incorporated

D Total assets (see Specific Instructions)

E Check applicable boxes: (1) ☐ Initial return (2) ☐ Final return (3) ☐ Change of address $

Income				
1a	Gross receipts or sales |_____ **b** Less returns and allowances |_____ **c** Bal ▶	1c	
2	Cost of goods sold (Schedule A, line 8)		2	
3	Gross profit. Subtract line 2 from line 1c		3	
4	Dividends (Schedule C, line 19)		4	
5	Interest		5	
6	Gross rents		6	
7	Gross royalties		7	
8	Capital gain net income (attach Schedule D (Form 1120))		8	
9	Net gain or (loss) from Form 4797, Part II, line 20 (attach Form 4797)		9	
10	Other income (see instructions—attach schedule)		10	
11	**Total income.** Add lines 3 through 10 ▶		11	

Deductions (See instructions for limitations on deductions.)				
12	Compensation of officers (Schedule E, line 4)		12	
13a	Salaries and wages |_____ **b** Less employment credits |_____ **c** Bal ▶	13c	
14	Repairs and maintenance		14	
15	Bad debts		15	
16	Rents		16	
17	Taxes and licenses		17	
18	Interest		18	
19	Charitable contributions (see instructions for 10% limitation)		19	
20	Depreciation (attach Form 4562)	20		
21	Less depreciation claimed on Schedule A and elsewhere on return	21a	21b	
22	Depletion		22	
23	Advertising		23	
24	Pension, profit-sharing, etc., plans		24	
25	Employee benefit programs		25	
26	Other deductions (attach schedule)		26	
27	**Total deductions.** Add lines 12 through 26 ▶		27	
28	Taxable income before net operating loss deduction and special deductions. Subtract line 27 from line 11		28	
29	**Less: a** Net operating loss deduction (see instructions)	29a		
	b Special deductions (Schedule C, line 20)	29b	29c	

Tax and Payments				
30	**Taxable income.** Subtract line 29c from line 28		30	
31	**Total tax** (Schedule J, line 10)		31	
32	Payments: **a** 1992 overpayment credited to 1993	32a		
b	1993 estimated tax payments	32b		
c	Less 1993 refund applied for on Form 4466	32c ( ) **d** Bal ▶	32d	
e	Tax deposited with Form 7004		32e	
f	Credit from regulated investment companies (attach Form 2439)		32f	
g	Credit for Federal tax on fuels (attach Form 4136). See instructions		32g	32h	
33	Estimated tax penalty (see instructions). Check if Form 2220 is attached ▶ ☐		33	
34	**Tax due.** If line 32h is smaller than the total of lines 31 and 33, enter amount owed		34	
35	**Overpayment.** If line 32h is larger than the total of lines 31 and 33, enter amount overpaid		35	
36	Enter amount of line 35 you want: **Credited to 1994 estimated tax** ▶ **Refunded** ▶		36	

Please Sign Here

Under penalties of perjury, I declare that I have examined this return, including accompanying schedules and statements, and to the best of my knowledge and belief, it is true, correct, and complete. Declaration of preparer (other than taxpayer) is based on all information of which preparer has any knowledge.

▶ Signature of officer   Date   ▶ Title

Paid Preparer's Use Only

Preparer's signature ▶	Date	Check if self-employed ☐	Preparer's social security number
Firm's name (or yours if self-employed) and address ▶		E.I. No. ▶	
		ZIP code ▶	

Cat. No. 11450Q

Form 1120 (1993)   Page **2**

Schedule A | Cost of Goods Sold (See instructions.)

1	Inventory at beginning of year	**1**
2	Purchases	**2**
3	Cost of labor	**3**
4	Additional section 263A costs (attach schedule)	**4**
5	Other costs (attach schedule)	**5**
6	**Total.** Add lines 1 through 5	**6**
7	Inventory at end of year	**7**
8	**Cost of goods sold.** Subtract line 7 from line 6. Enter here and on page 1, line 2	**8**

9a Check all methods used for valuing closing inventory:
    ☐ Cost   ☐ Lower of cost or market as described in Regulations section 1.471-4
    ☐ Writedown of subnormal goods as described in Regulations section 1.471-2(c)
    ☐ Other (Specify method used and attach explanation.) ▶ ....

  b Check if the LIFO inventory method was adopted this tax year for any goods (if checked, attach Form 970) . . . . . ▶ ☐

  c If the LIFO inventory method was used for this tax year, enter percentage (or amounts) of closing
     inventory computed under LIFO **9c**

  d Do the rules of section 263A (for property produced or acquired for resale) apply to the corporation? . . . . . ☐ Yes ☐ No

  e Was there any change in determining quantities, cost, or valuations between opening and closing inventory? If "Yes,"
     attach explanation . . . . ☐ Yes ☐ No

Schedule C | Dividends and Special Deductions (See instructions.)

		(a) Dividends received	(b) %	(c) Special deductions (a) × (b)
1	Dividends from less-than-20%-owned domestic corporations that are subject to the 70% deduction (other than debt-financed stock)		70	
2	Dividends from 20%-or-more-owned domestic corporations that are subject to the 80% deduction (other than debt-financed stock)		80	
3	Dividends on debt-financed stock of domestic and foreign corporations (section 246A)		see instructions	
4	Dividends on certain preferred stock of less-than-20%-owned public utilities . . .		42	
5	Dividends on certain preferred stock of 20%-or-more-owned public utilities . . .		48	
6	Dividends from less-than-20%-owned foreign corporations and certain FSCs that are subject to the 70% deduction		70	
7	Dividends from 20%-or-more-owned foreign corporations and certain FSCs that are subject to the 80% deduction		80	
8	Dividends from wholly owned foreign subsidiaries subject to the 100% deduction (section 245(b))		100	
9	**Total.** Add lines 1 through 8. See instructions for limitation			
10	Dividends from domestic corporations received by a small business investment company operating under the Small Business Investment Act of 1958		100	
11	Dividends from certain FSCs that are subject to the 100% deduction (section 245(c)(1))		100	
12	Dividends from affiliated group members subject to the 100% deduction (section 243(a)(3))		100	
13	Other dividends from foreign corporations not included on lines 3, 6, 7, 8, or 11 . .			
14	Income from controlled foreign corporations under subpart F (attach Form(s) 5471) .			
15	Foreign dividend gross-up (section 78)			
16	IC-DISC and former DISC dividends not included on lines 1, 2, or 3 (section 246(d)) .			
17	Other dividends			
18	Deduction for dividends paid on certain preferred stock of public utilities (see instructions)			
19	**Total dividends.** Add lines 1 through 17. Enter here and on line 4, page 1 . ▶			
20	**Total special deductions.** Add lines 9, 10, 11, 12, and 18. Enter here and on line 29b, page 1 . . . . . ▶			

Schedule E | Compensation of Officers (See instructions for line 12, page 1.)

Complete Schedule E only if total receipts (line 1a plus lines 4 through 10 on page 1, Form 1120) are $500,000 or more.

	(a) Name of officer	(b) Social security number	(c) Percent of time devoted to business	Percent of corporation stock owned		(f) Amount of compensation
				(d) Common	(e) Preferred	
1			%	%	%	
			%	%	%	
			%	%	%	
			%	%	%	
			%	%	%	

2	Total compensation of officers	
3	Compensation of officers claimed on Schedule A and elsewhere on return	
4	Subtract line 3 from line 2. Enter the result here and on line 12, page 1	

Form 1120 (1993)   Page **3**

Schedule J — Tax Computation (See instructions.)

1 Check if the corporation is a member of a controlled group (see sections 1561 and 1563) . . . . . ▶ ☐

2a If the box on line 1 is checked, enter the corporation's share of the $50,000, $25,000, and $9,925,000 taxable income brackets (in that order):

(1) ☐ $ _____   (2) ☐ $ _____   (3) ☐ $ _____

b Enter the corporation's share of:

(1) additional 5% tax (not more than $11,750) . . . ☐ $ _____

(2) additional 3% tax (not more than $100,000) . . ☐ $ _____

3 Income tax. Check this box if the corporation is a qualified personal service corporation as defined in section 448(d)(2) (see instructions on page 15). . . . . ▶ ☐ | **3** |

4a	Foreign tax credit (attach Form 1118)	**4a**	
b	Possessions tax credit (attach Form 5735)	**4b**	
c	Orphan drug credit (attach Form 6765)	**4c**	
d	Check: ☐ Nonconventional source fuel credit ☐ QEV credit (attach Form 8834)	**4d**	

e General business credit. Enter here and check which forms are attached:

☐ Form 3800 ☐ Form 3468 ☐ Form 5884 ☐ Form 6478 ☐ Form 6765

☐ Form 8586 ☐ Form 8830 ☐ Form 8826 ☐ Form 8835 . . . . | **4e** |

f Credit for prior year minimum tax (attach Form 8827) . . . . | **4f** |

5	**Total credits.** Add lines 4a through 4f	**5**
6	Subtract line 5 from line 3	**6**
7	Personal holding company tax (attach Schedule PH (Form 1120))	**7**
8	Recapture taxes. Check if from: ☐ Form 4255 ☐ Form 8611	**8**
9a	Alternative minimum tax (attach Form 4626)	**9a**
b	Environmental tax (attach Form 4626)	**9b**
10	**Total tax.** Add lines 6 through 9b. Enter here and on line 31, page 1	**10**

Schedule K — Other Information (See pages 17 and 18 of instructions.)

	Yes	No
1 Check method of accounting: **a** ☐ Cash		
b ☐ Accrual **c** ☐ Other (specify) ▶		

2 Refer to page 19 of the instructions and state the principal:

a Business activity code no. ▶ ....

b Business activity ▶ ....

c Product or service ▶ ....

3 Did the corporation at the end of the tax year own, directly or indirectly, 50% or more of the voting stock of a domestic corporation? (For rules of attribution, see section 267(c).) . . . . . .

If "Yes," attach a schedule showing: (a) name and identifying number, (b) percentage owned, and (c) taxable income or (loss) before NOL and special deductions of such corporation for the tax year ending with or within your tax year.

4 Is the corporation a subsidiary in an affiliated group or a parent-subsidiary controlled group? . . . . . .

If "Yes," enter employer identification number and name of the parent corporation ▶ ....

....

5 Did any individual, partnership, corporation, estate or trust at the end of the tax year own, directly or indirectly, 50% or more of the corporation's voting stock? (For rules of attribution, see section 267(c).) . . . . . .

If "Yes," attach a schedule showing name and identifying number. (Do not include any information already entered in **4** above.) Enter percentage owned ▶ ....

6 During this tax year, did the corporation pay dividends (other than stock dividends and distributions in exchange for stock) in excess of the corporation's current and accumulated earnings and profits? (See secs. 301 and 316.) . . . .

If "Yes," file Form 5452. If this is a consolidated return, answer here for the parent corporation and on **Form 851,** Affiliations Schedule, for each subsidiary.

	Yes	No
7 Was the corporation a U.S. shareholder of any controlled foreign corporation? (See sections 951 and 957.) . . .		

If "Yes," attach Form 5471 for each such corporation. Enter number of Forms 5471 attached ▶ ....

8 At any time during the 1993 calendar year, did the corporation have an interest in or a signature or other authority over a financial account in a foreign country (such as a bank account, securities account, or other financial account)? .

If "Yes," the corporation may have to file Form TD F 90-22.1.

If "Yes," enter name of foreign country ▶ ....

9 Was the corporation the grantor of, or transferor to, a foreign trust that existed during the current tax year, whether or not the corporation has any beneficial interest in it? If "Yes," the corporation may have to file Forms 926, 3520, or 3520-A

10 Did one foreign person at any time during the tax year own, directly or indirectly, at least 25% of: (a) the total voting power of all classes of stock of the corporation entitled to vote, or (b) the total value of all classes of stock of the corporation? If "Yes,"

a Enter percentage owned ▶ ....

b Enter owner's country ▶ ....

c The corporation may have to file Form 5472. Enter number of Forms 5472 attached ▶ ....

11 Check this box if the corporation issued publicly offered debt instruments with original issue discount . ▶ ☐

If so, the corporation may have to file Form 8281.

12 Enter the amount of tax-exempt interest received or accrued during the tax year ▶ $ ....

13 If there were 35 or fewer shareholders at the end of the tax year, enter the number ▶ ....

14 If the corporation has an NOL for the tax year and is electing to forego the carryback period, check here ▶ ☐

15 Enter the available NOL carryover from prior tax years (Do not reduce it by any deduction on line 29a.) ▶ $

Form 1120 (1993)

Schedule L	Balance Sheets	Beginning of tax year		End of tax year	
	Assets	(a)	(b)	(c)	(d)
1	Cash				
2a	Trade notes and accounts receivable	( )		( )	
b	Less allowance for bad debts	( )		( )	
3	Inventories				
4	U.S. government obligations				
5	Tax-exempt securities (see instructions)				
6	Other current assets (attach schedule)				
7	Loans to stockholders				
8	Mortgage and real estate loans				
9	Other investments (attach schedule)				
10a	Buildings and other depreciable assets				
b	Less accumulated depreciation	( )		( )	
11a	Depletable assets				
b	Less accumulated depletion	( )		( )	
12	Land (net of any amortization)				
13a	Intangible assets (amortizable only)				
b	Less accumulated amortization	( )		( )	
14	Other assets (attach schedule)				
15	Total assets				
	Liabilities and Stockholders' Equity				
16	Accounts payable				
17	Mortgages, notes, bonds payable in less than 1 year				
18	Other current liabilities (attach schedule)				
19	Loans from stockholders				
20	Mortgages, notes, bonds payable in 1 year or more				
21	Other liabilities (attach schedule)				
22	Capital stock: a Preferred stock				
	b Common stock				
23	Paid-in or capital surplus				
24	Retained earnings—Appropriated (attach schedule)				
25	Retained earnings—Unappropriated				
26	Less cost of treasury stock		( )		( )
27	Total liabilities and stockholders' equity				

Note: *You are not required to complete Schedules M-1 and M-2 below if the total assets on line 15, column (d) of Schedule L are less than $25,000.*

Schedule M-1	Reconciliation of Income (Loss) per Books With Income per Return (See instructions.)

1	Net income (loss) per books		7	Income recorded on books this year not included on this return (itemize):	
2	Federal income tax			Tax-exempt interest $	
3	Excess of capital losses over capital gains			....	
4	Income subject to tax not recorded on books this year (itemize):		8	Deductions on this return not charged against book income this year (itemize):	
	....		a	Depreciation . . . . $	
5	Expenses recorded on books this year not deducted on this return (itemize):		b	Contributions carryover $	
a	Depreciation . . . . $			....	
b	Contributions carryover $			....	
c	Travel and entertainment $				
	....		9	Add lines 7 and 8	
	....		10	Income (line 28, page 1)—line 6 less line 9	
6	Add lines 1 through 5				

Schedule M-2	Analysis of Unappropriated Retained Earnings per Books (Line 25, Schedule L)

1	Balance at beginning of year		5	Distributions: a Cash	
2	Net income (loss) per books			b Stock	
3	Other increases (itemize):			c Property	
	....		6	Other decreases (itemize):	
	....			....	
	....		7	Add lines 5 and 6	
4	Add lines 1, 2, and 3		8	Balance at end of year (line 4 less line 7)	

♻ *Printed on recycled paper*

*U.S. Government Printing Office: 1994 — 301-628/00122

Form **1120S** Department of the Treasury Internal Revenue Service	**U.S. Income Tax Return for an S Corporation** ▶ **Do not file this form unless the corporation has timely filed Form 2553 to elect to be an S corporation.** ▶ **See separate instructions.**	OMB No. 1545-0130 **1993**

For calendar year 1993, or tax year beginning ...., 1993, and ending ...., 19 .....

A Date of election as an S corporation **B** Business code no. (see Specific Instructions)	**Use IRS label. Other- wise, please print or type.**	Name Number, street, and room or suite no. (If a P.O. box, see page 9 of the instructions.) City or town, state, and ZIP code	**C Employer identification number** **D Date incorporated** **E** Total assets (see Specific Instructions) $

F Check applicable boxes: (1) ☐ Initial return　(2) ☐ Final return　(3) ☐ Change in address　(4) ☐ Amended return

G Check this box if this S corporation is subject to the consolidated audit procedures of sections 6241 through 6245 (see instructions before checking this box) . ▶ ☐

H Enter number of shareholders in the corporation at end of the tax year . . . . ▶

Caution: *Include **only** trade or business income and expenses on lines 1a through 21. See the instructions for more information.*

Income	**1a** Gross receipts or sales [＿＿＿] **b** Less returns and allowances [＿＿＿] **c** Bal ▶	**1c**	
	2 Cost of goods sold (Schedule A, line 8)	**2**	
	3 Gross profit. Subtract line 2 from line 1c	**3**	
	4 Net gain (loss) from Form 4797, Part II, line 20 *(attach Form 4797)* .	**4**	
	5 Other income (loss) (see instructions) *(attach schedule)*	**5**	
	6 **Total income (loss).** Combine lines 3 through 5 . . . . . . ▶	**6**	

Deductions (See instructions for limitations.)	**7** Compensation of officers	**7**	
	8a Salaries and wages [＿＿＿] **b** Less employment credits [＿＿＿] **c** Bal ▶	**8c**	
	9 Repairs and maintenance.	**9**	
	10 Bad debts	**10**	
	11 Rents	**11**	
	12 Taxes and licenses.	**12**	
	13 Interest	**13**	
	14a Depreciation (see instructions) . . . . |**14a**|		
	b Depreciation claimed on Schedule A and elsewhere on return . |**14b**|		
	c Subtract line 14b from line 14a	**14c**	
	15 Depletion **(Do not deduct oil and gas depletion.)**	**15**	
	16 Advertising	**16**	
	17 Pension, profit-sharing, etc., plans	**17**	
	18 Employee benefit programs	**18**	
	19 Other deductions (see instructions) *(attach schedule)*	**19**	
	20 **Total deductions.** Add lines 7 through 19 . . . . ▶	**20**	
	21 Ordinary income (loss) from trade or business activities. Subtract line 20 from line 6	**21**	

Tax and Payments	**22** **Tax: a** Excess net passive income tax *(attach schedule)*. . . |**22a**|		
	b Tax from Schedule D (Form 1120S) . . . . |**22b**|		
	c Add lines 22a and 22b (see instructions for additional taxes) . .	**22c**	
	23 **Payments: a** 1993 estimated tax payments. . . . . . . |**23a**|		
	b Tax deposited with Form 7004 . . . . |**23b**|		
	c Credit for Federal tax paid on fuels *(attach Form 4136)* . . . |**23c**|		
	d Add lines 23a through 23c	**23d**	
	24 Estimated tax penalty (see instructions). Check if Form 2220 is attached. . . . . . ▶☐	**24**	
	25 **Tax due.** If the total of lines 22c and 24 is larger than line 23d, enter amount owed. See instructions for depositary method of payment	**25**	
	26 **Overpayment.** If line 23d is larger than the total of lines 22c and 24, enter amount overpaid ▶	**26**	
	27 Enter amount of line 26 you want: **Credited to 1994 estimated tax** ▶ [＿＿＿] **Refunded** ▶	**27**	

**Please
Sign
Here**

Under penalties of perjury, I declare that I have examined this return, including accompanying schedules and statements, and to the best of my knowledge and belief, it is true, correct, and complete. Declaration of preparer (other than taxpayer) is based on all information of which preparer has any knowledge.

▶ _____   _____   ▶ _____
   Signature of officer   Date   Title

Paid Preparer's Use Only	Preparer's signature ▶	Date	Check if self- employed ▶ ☐	Preparer's social security number
	Firm's name (or yours if self-employed) and address ▶		E.I. No. ▶	
			ZIP code ▶	

For Paperwork Reduction Act Notice, see page 1 of separate instructions.   Cat. No. 11510H   Form **1120S** (1993)

Form 1120S (1993)   Page **2**

Schedule A	**Cost of Goods Sold** (See instructions.)			

1	Inventory at beginning of year	**1**	
2	Purchases.	**2**	
3	Cost of labor.	**3**	
4	Additional section 263A costs (see instructions) *(attach schedule)*	**4**	
5	Other costs *(attach schedule)*.	**5**	
6	**Total.** Add lines 1 through 5.	**6**	
7	Inventory at end of year	**7**	
8	**Cost of goods sold.** Subtract line 7 from line 6. Enter here and on page 1, line 2	**8**	

9a Check all methods used for valuing closing inventory:

(i) ☐ Cost

(ii) ☐ Lower of cost or market as described in Regulations section 1.471-4

(iii) ☐ Writedown of "subnormal" goods as described in Regulations section 1.471-2(c)

(iv) ☐ Other (specify method used and attach explanation) ▶ ....

b Check if the LIFO inventory method was adopted this tax year for any goods *(if checked, attach Form 970)*. . . . . ▶ ☐

c If the LIFO inventory method was used for this tax year, enter percentage (or amounts) of closing
inventory computed under LIFO . . . . | **9c** | |

d Do the rules of section 263A (for property produced or acquired for resale) apply to the corporation? . . . . ☐ Yes ☐ No

e Was there any change in determining quantities, cost, or valuations between opening and closing inventory? . . ☐ Yes ☐ No
If "Yes," attach explanation.

Schedule B	**Other Information**		

		Yes	No
1	Check method of accounting: **(a)** ☐ Cash **(b)** ☐ Accrual **(c)** ☐ Other (specify) ▶		
2	Refer to the list in the instructions and state the corporation's principal: **(a)** Business activity ▶ .... **(b)** Product or service ▶		
3	Did the corporation at the end of the tax year own, directly or indirectly, 50% or more of the voting stock of a domestic corporation? (For rules of attribution, see section 267(c).) If "Yes," attach a schedule showing: **(a)** name, address, and employer identification number and **(b)** percentage owned.		
4	Was the corporation a member of a controlled group subject to the provisions of section 1561?		
5	At any time during calendar year 1993, did the corporation have an interest in or a signature or other authority over a financial account in a foreign country (such as a bank account, securities account, or other financial account)? (See instructions for exceptions and filing requirements for Form TD F 90-22.1.) If "Yes," enter the name of the foreign country ▶		
6	Was the corporation the grantor of, or transferor to, a foreign trust that existed during the current tax year, whether or not the corporation has any beneficial interest in it? If "Yes," the corporation may have to file Forms 3520, 3520-A, or 926 .		
7	Check this box if the corporation has filed or is required to file **Form 8264**, Application for Registration of a Tax Shelter . . . . ▶ ☐		
8	Check this box if the corporation issued publicly offered debt instruments with original issue discount . . ▶ ☐ If so, the corporation may have to file **Form 8281**, Information Return for Publicly Offered Original Issue Discount Instruments.		
9	If the corporation: **(a)** filed its election to be an S corporation after 1986, **(b)** was a C corporation before it elected to be an S corporation **or** the corporation acquired an asset with a basis determined by reference to its basis (or the basis of any other property) in the hands of a C corporation, and **(c)** has net unrealized built-in gain (defined in section 1374(d)(1)) in excess of the net recognized built-in gain from prior years, enter the net unrealized built-in gain reduced by net recognized built-in gain from prior years (see instructions) . . . . . ▶ $		
10	Check this box if the corporation had subchapter C earnings and profits at the close of the tax year (see instructions) . . . . ▶ ☐		

Designation of Tax Matters Person (See instructions.)

Enter below the shareholder designated as the tax matters person (TMP) for the tax year of this return:

Name of designated TMP ▶	Identifying number of TMP ▶
Address of designated TMP ▶	

Form 1120S (1993)   Page **3**

Schedule K — Shareholders' Shares of Income, Credits, Deductions, etc.

	(a) Pro rata share items		(b) Total amount	

Income (Loss)

1	Ordinary income (loss) from trade or business activities (page 1, line 21)	**1**	
2	Net income (loss) from rental real estate activities (attach Form 8825)	**2**	
3a	Gross income from other rental activities **3a**		
b	Expenses from other rental activities (attach schedule). **3b**		
c	Net income (loss) from other rental activities. Subtract line 3b from line 3a	**3c**	
4	Portfolio income (loss):		
a	Interest income	**4a**	
b	Dividend income.	**4b**	
c	Royalty income	**4c**	
d	Net short-term capital gain (loss) (attach Schedule D (Form 1120S))	**4d**	
e	Net long-term capital gain (loss) (attach Schedule D (Form 1120S)).	**4e**	
f	Other portfolio income (loss) (attach schedule)	**4f**	
5	Net gain (loss) under section 1231 (other than due to casualty or theft) (attach Form 4797)	**5**	
6	Other income (loss) (attach schedule)	**6**	

Deductions

7	Charitable contributions (see instructions) (attach schedule)	**7**	
8	Section 179 expense deduction (attach Form 4562).	**8**	
9	Deductions related to portfolio income (loss) (see instructions) (itemize)	**9**	
10	Other deductions (attach schedule)	**10**	

Investment Interest

11a	Interest expense on investment debts	**11a**	
b (1)	Investment income included on lines 4a, 4b, 4c, and 4f above	**11b(1)**	
(2)	Investment expenses included on line 9 above	**11b(2)**	

Credits

12a	Credit for alcohol used as a fuel (attach Form 6478)	**12a**	
b	Low-income housing credit (see instructions):		
(1)	From partnerships to which section 42(j)(5) applies for property placed in service before 1990	**12b(1)**	
(2)	Other than on line 12b(1) for property placed in service before 1990.	**12b(2)**	
(3)	From partnerships to which section 42(j)(5) applies for property placed in service after 1989	**12b(3)**	
(4)	Other than on line 12b(3) for property placed in service after 1989	**12b(4)**	
c	Qualified rehabilitation expenditures related to rental real estate activities (attach Form 3468) .	**12c**	
d	Credits (other than credits shown on lines 12b and 12c) related to rental real estate activities (see instructions).	**12d**	
e	Credits related to other rental activities (see instructions)	**12e**	
13	Other credits (see instructions)	**13**	

Adjustments and Tax Preference Items

14a	Depreciation adjustment on property placed in service after 1986	**14a**	
b	Adjusted gain or loss	**14b**	
c	Depletion (other than oil and gas)	**14c**	
d (1)	Gross income from oil, gas, or geothermal properties	**14d(1)**	
(2)	Deductions allocable to oil, gas, or geothermal properties	**14d(2)**	
e	Other adjustments and tax preference items (attach schedule)	**14e**	

Foreign Taxes

15a	Type of income ▶..		
b	Name of foreign country or U.S. possession ▶.............................		
c	Total gross income from sources outside the United States (attach schedule)	**15c**	
d	Total applicable deductions and losses (attach schedule)	**15d**	
e	Total foreign taxes (check one): ▶ ☐ Paid ☐ Accrued	**15e**	
f	Reduction in taxes available for credit (attach schedule)	**15f**	
g	Other foreign tax information (attach schedule)	**15g**	

Other

16a	Total expenditures to which a section 59(e) election may apply	**16a**	
b	Type of expenditures ▶..		
17	Tax-exempt interest income	**17**	
18	Other tax-exempt income	**18**	
19	Nondeductible expenses	**19**	
20	Total property distributions (including cash) other than dividends reported on line 22 below	**20**	
21	Other items and amounts required to be reported separately to shareholders (see instructions) (attach schedule)		
22	Total dividend distributions paid from accumulated earnings and profits	**22**	
23	**Income (loss).** (Required only if Schedule M-1 must be completed.) Combine lines 1 through 6 in column (b). From the result, subtract the sum of lines 7 through 11a, 15e, and 16a	**23**	

208

Form 1120S (1993) Page **4**

Schedule L Balance Sheets

Assets	Beginning of tax year (a)	(b)	End of tax year (c)	(d)
1 Cash				
2a Trade notes and accounts receivable				
b Less allowance for bad debts				
3 Inventories				
4 U.S. Government obligations				
5 Tax-exempt securities				
6 Other current assets (attach schedule)				
7 Loans to shareholders				
8 Mortgage and real estate loans				
9 Other investments (attach schedule)				
10a Buildings and other depreciable assets				
b Less accumulated depreciation				
11a Depletable assets				
b Less accumulated depletion				
12 Land (net of any amortization)				
13a Intangible assets (amortizable only)				
b Less accumulated amortization				
14 Other assets (attach schedule)				
15 Total assets				
Liabilities and Shareholders' Equity				
16 Accounts payable				
17 Mortgages, notes, bonds payable in less than 1 year				
18 Other current liabilities (attach schedule)				
19 Loans from shareholders				
20 Mortgages, notes, bonds payable in 1 year or more				
21 Other liabilities (attach schedule)				
22 Capital stock				
23 Paid-in or capital surplus				
24 Retained earnings				
25 Less cost of treasury stock		( )		( )
26 Total liabilities and shareholders' equity				

Schedule M-1 Reconciliation of Income (Loss) per Books With Income (Loss) per Return (You are not required to complete this schedule if the total assets on line 15, column (d), of Schedule L are less than $25,000.)

1 Net income (loss) per books

2 Income included on Schedule K, lines 1 through 6, not recorded on books this year (itemize): ....

3 Expenses recorded on books this year not included on Schedule K, lines 1 through 11a, 15e, and 16a (itemize):

a Depreciation $ ....

b Travel and entertainment $ ....

4 Add lines 1 through 3

5 Income recorded on books this year not included on Schedule K, lines 1 through 6 (itemize):

a Tax-exempt interest $ ....

6 Deductions included on Schedule K, lines 1 through 11a, 15e, and 16a, not charged against book income this year (itemize):

a Depreciation $ ....

7 Add lines 5 and 6

8 Income (loss) (Schedule K, line 23). Line 4 less line 7

Schedule M-2 Analysis of Accumulated Adjustments Account, Other Adjustments Account, and Shareholders' Undistributed Taxable Income Previously Taxed (See instructions.)

	(a) Accumulated adjustments account	(b) Other adjustments account	(c) Shareholders' undistributed taxable income previously taxed
1 Balance at beginning of tax year			
2 Ordinary income from page 1, line 21			
3 Other additions			
4 Loss from page 1, line 21	( )		
5 Other reductions	( )	( )	
6 Combine lines 1 through 5			
7 Distributions other than dividend distributions			
8 Balance at end of tax year. Subtract line 7 from line 6			

*U.S. Government Printing Office: 1993 — 345-315

209

Form 1120-A

Department of the Treasury
Internal Revenue Service

U.S. Corporation Short-Form Income Tax Return

See separate instructions to make sure the corporation qualifies to file Form 1120-A.

For calendar year 1993 or tax year beginning ...., 1993, ending.............., 19.....

OMB No. 1545-0890

1993

Check this box if the corp. is a personal service corp. (as defined in Temporary Regs. section 1.441-4T—see instructions) ▶ ☐	**Use IRS label. Other-wise, please print or type.**	Name
		Number, street, and room or suite no. (If a P.O. box, see page 7 of instructions.)
		City or town, state, and ZIP code

B Employer identification number

C Date incorporated

D Total assets (see Specific Instructions)
$

E Check applicable boxes: **(1)** ☐ Initial return **(2)** ☐ Change of address

F Check method of accounting: **(1)** ☐ Cash **(2)** ☐ Accrual **(3)** ☐ Other (specify) . . ▶

Income

1a	Gross receipts or sales [____] **b** Less returns and allowances [____] **c** Balance ▶	1c	
2	Cost of goods sold (see instructions)	2	
3	Gross profit. Subtract line 2 from line 1c	3	
4	Domestic corporation dividends subject to the 70% deduction	4	
5	Interest	5	
6	Gross rents	6	
7	Gross royalties	7	
8	Capital gain net income (attach Schedule D (Form 1120)) . . .	8	
9	Net gain or (loss) from Form 4797, Part II, line 20 (attach Form 4797)	9	
10	Other income (see instructions)	10	
11	**Total income.** Add lines 3 through 10 . . . . ▶	11	

Deductions
(See instructions for limitations on deductions.)

12	Compensation of officers (see instructions)	12	
13a	Salaries and wages [____] **b** Less employment credits [____] **c** Bal ▶	13c	
14	Repairs and maintenance	14	
15	Bad debts	15	
16	Rents	16	
17	Taxes and licenses	17	
18	Interest	18	
19	Charitable contributions (see instructions for 10% limitation) . .	19	
20	Depreciation (attach Form 4562) . . . . `20`		
21	Less depreciation claimed elsewhere on return . . . . . `21a`	21b	
22	Other deductions (attach schedule)	22	
23	**Total deductions.** Add lines 12 through 22 . . . . . . ▶	23	
24	Taxable income before net operating loss deduction and special deductions. Subtract line 23 from line 11	24	
25	**Less: a** Net operating loss deduction (see instructions) . . . . `25a`		
	b Special deductions (see instructions) . . . . `25b`	25c	

Tax and Payments

26	**Taxable income.** Subtract line 25c from line 24	26	
27	**Total tax** (from page 2, Part I, line 7)	27	
28	**Payments:**		
a	1992 overpayment credited to 1993 `28a`		
b	1993 estimated tax payments `28b`		
c	Less 1993 refund applied for on Form 4466 `28c` ( ) Bal ▶ `28d`		
e	Tax deposited with Form 7004 . . . . `28e`		
f	Credit from regulated investment companies (attach Form 2439) . `28f`		
g	Credit for Federal tax on fuels (attach Form 4136). See instructions . `28g`		
h	**Total payments.** Add lines 28d through 28g	28h	
29	Estimated tax penalty (see instructions). Check if Form 2220 is attached . . . . . ▶ ☐	29	
30	**Tax due.** If line 28h is smaller than the total of lines 27 and 29, enter amount owed	30	
31	**Overpayment.** If line 28h is larger than the total of lines 27 and 29, enter amount overpaid . . .	31	
32	Enter amount of line 31 you want: **Credited to 1994 estimated tax** ▶ _____ **Refunded** ▶	32	

Please Sign Here

Under penalties of perjury, I declare that I have examined this return, including accompanying schedules and statements, and to the best of my knowledge and belief, it is true, correct, and complete. Declaration of preparer (other than taxpayer) is based on all information of which preparer has any knowledge.

▶ _____ Signature of officer ____ Date ____ ▶ _____ Title

Paid Preparer's Use Only	Preparer's signature ▶	Date	Check if self-employed ▶ ☐	Preparer's social security number
	Firm's name (or yours if self-employed) and address ▶		E.I. No. ▶	
			ZIP code ▶	

For Paperwork Reduction Act Notice, see page 1 of the instructions.

Cat. No. 11456E

Form **1120-A** (1993)

Form 1120-A (1993)   Page **2**

Part I	Tax Computation (See instructions.)		

1 Income tax. Check this box if the corporation is a qualified personal service corporation as defined in section 448(d)(2) (see instructions on page 15) . . . . ▶ ☐   **1**

2a General business credit. Check if from: ☐ Form 3800 ☐ Form 3468 ☐ Form 5884
☐ Form 6478 ☐ Form 6765 ☐ Form 8586 ☐ Form 8830 ☐ Form 8826 ☐ Form 8835   **2a**

b Credit for prior year minimum tax (attach Form 8827) **2b**

3 **Total credits.** Add lines 2a and 2b **3**

4 Subtract line 3 from line 1 . . . .   **4**

5 Recapture taxes. Check if from: ☐ Form 4255 ☐ Form 8611 . . . . .   **5**

6 Alternative minimum tax (attach Form 4626) **6**

7 **Total tax.** Add lines 4 through 6. Enter here and on line 27, page 1 . . . .   **7**

Part II	Other Information (See instructions.)		

1 Refer to page 19 of the instructions and state the principal:

a Business activity code no. ▶ ....

b Business activity ▶ ....

c Product or service ▶ ....

2 Did any individual, partnership, estate, or trust at the end of the tax year own, directly or indirectly, 50% or more of the corporation's voting stock? (For rules of attribution, see section 267(c).) . . . . ☐ Yes ☐ No

If "Yes," attach a schedule showing name and identifying number.

3 Enter the amount of tax-exempt interest received or accrued during the tax year . . . . ▶ |$ |

4 Enter amount of cash distributions and the book value of property (other than cash) distributions made in this tax year . . . . ▶ |$ |

5a If an amount is entered on line 2, page 1, see the worksheet on page 13 for amounts to enter below:

(1) Purchases . . . .

(2) Additional sec. 263A costs (see instructions—attach schedule) .

(3) Other costs (attach schedule) .

b Do the rules of section 263A (for property produced or acquired for resale) apply to the corporation? . . . . . . ☐ Yes ☐ No

6 At any time during the 1993 calendar year, did the corporation have an interest in or a signature or other authority over a financial account in a foreign country (such as a bank account, securities account, or other financial account)? If "Yes," the corporation may have to file Form TD F 90-22.1 . . . . ☐ Yes ☐ No
If "Yes," enter the name of the foreign country ▶ ....

Part III	Balance Sheets		(a) Beginning of tax year		(b) End of tax year	

Assets

1	Cash					
2a	Trade notes and accounts receivable					
b	Less allowance for bad debts	(	)	(		)
3	Inventories					
4	U.S. government obligations					
5	Tax-exempt securities (see instructions)					
6	Other current assets (attach schedule)					
7	Loans to stockholders					
8	Mortgage and real estate loans					
9a	Depreciable, depletable, and intangible assets . . .					
b	Less accumulated depreciation, depletion, and amortization	(	)	(		)
10	Land (net of any amortization)					
11	Other assets (attach schedule)					
12	Total assets					

Liabilities and Stockholders' Equity

13	Accounts payable					
14	Other current liabilities (attach schedule)					
15	Loans from stockholders					
16	Mortgages, notes, bonds payable					
17	Other liabilities (attach schedule)					
18	Capital stock (preferred and common stock) . . .					
19	Paid-in or capital surplus					
20	Retained earnings					
21	Less cost of treasury stock	(	)	(		)
22	Total liabilities and stockholders' equity					

Part IV	Reconciliation of Income (Loss) per Books With Income per Return *(You are not required to complete Part IV if the total assets on line 12, column (b), Part III are less than $25,000.)*

1 Net income (loss) per books . . . . . .

2 Federal income tax . . . .

3 Excess of capital losses over capital gains . .

4 Income subject to tax not recorded on books this year (itemize) ....

5 Expenses recorded on books this year not deducted on this return (itemize)

6 Income recorded on books this year not included on this return (itemize) ....

7 Deductions on this return not charged against book income this year (itemize) ....

8 Income (line 24, page 1). Enter the sum of lines 1 through 5 less the sum of lines 6 and 7 . . . .

✲ *Printed on recycled paper*

Chapter 15

Dissolving a Corporation

The act of dissolving a corporation is generally based on a decision to stop the active business activities of the corporation. Dissolutions can be voluntarily adopted by the shareholders and directors of a corporation. Dissolutions can also be involuntary. Involuntary dissolution may be caused by the revocation of the corporate Articles of Incorporation by the state for failure to file the proper reports, pay the proper taxes, or maintain a registered office and agent. Bankruptcy of the corporation can also lead to involuntary dissolution of the business. Dissolution, as a major event in the life of a corporation, requires both shareholder and director approval. The action is generally initiated by the board of directors by an authorization and recommendation for dissolution, a proposal of a plan for dissolution, and a call for a special shareholders meeting. The shareholders must then approve the dissolution plan by majority vote and order the Secretary of the corporation to prepare and file the necessary Articles of Dissolution with the state corporation department. Upon acceptance of this document by the state, the corporation is officially dissolved. However, a corporation is allowed to continue to transact business for a short period after dissolution in order to wind up its affairs, liquidate its assets, and distribute proportionate shares of the corporate funds or property to its shareholders. During the period after the filing for dissolution, however, a corporation can not transact business which is not directed towards winding up its affairs, such as entering into long-term contracts. A Dissolution Checklist follows showing the steps necessary for a voluntary dissolution of a corporation. Please contact your state corporation department or an attorney for details of state requirements in your jurisdiction.

Dissolution Checklist

☐ The board of directors call for a special meeting regarding dissolution.

☐ Proper notice of the meeting (or waiver) is provided to all of the directors. (See Chapter 8).

☐ At the meeting, the board of directors adopts a resolution approving the dissolution of the corporation and calling for a special shareholders meeting. (A sample resolution is provided in this chapter).

☐ Proper notice of the meeting (or waiver) is provided to all of the shareholders of record. (See Chapter 9).

☐ At the shareholders meeting, a majority of the shareholders entitled to vote adopt a resolution approving the directors plan for dissolution and ordering the Secretary of the corporation to prepare and file Articles of Dissolution with the appropriate state corporation department. (A sample resolution is provided in this chapter).

☐ The Secretary prepares and files the Articles of Dissolution. (A sample Articles of Dissolution is provided in this chapter).

Resolution of the Board of Directors of _____
Approving Dissolution and Calling for Special Meeting

A meeting of the board of directors of this corporation was duly called and held on _____ , 19 ___ . A quorum of the board of directors was present and at the meeting it was decided, by majority vote, that it is advisable to dissolve this corporation

Therefore, it is
RESOLVED, that this corporation be dissolved as soon as is reasonably feasible, based upon the following plan for dissolution:

It is further
RESOLVED, that a special meeting of the shareholders of this corporation be held on _____ , 19 ___ at _____ m. at the offices of the corporation located at _____
for the purpose of obtaining shareholder approval of this recommendation for dissolution.

The Secretary is directed to give appropriate notice to all shareholders entitled to attend this meeting. The officers of this corporation are hereby authorized to perform all necessary acts to carry out this resolution.

The undersigned, _____ , certifies that he or she is the duly elected Secretary of this corporation and that the above is a true and correct copy of the resolution that was duly adopted at a meeting of the board of directors which was held in accordance with state law and the By-Laws of the corporation on _____ , 19 ___ . I further certify that such resolution is now in full force and effect.

Dated _____

Seal

_____
Secretary of the corporation

Resolution and Consent of the Shareholders of
_____ Approving Dissolution

A meeting of the shareholders of this corporation was duly called and held on _____ , 19 ___. A quorum of the shareholders was present, in person or by proxy, and at the meeting it was decided, by vote of holders of a majority of outstanding shares, that the it is in the best interests of this corporation that the corporation be dissolved.

Therefore, it is
RESOLVED, that this corporation be dissolved under the provisions of the following plan for dissolution:

Shareholders holding a majority of outstanding shares of stock in this corporation have signed this resolution and consent to this resolution. The Secretary of this corporation is authorized to prepare and execute official Articles of Dissolution and file and record these Articles of Dissolution as required. The officers of this corporation are authorized to perform all necessary acts to carry out this resolution.

Shareholder Name   Signature

_____   _____

_____   _____

_____   _____

_____   _____

_____   _____

_____   _____

_____   _____

_____   _____

The undersigned, _____ ,
certifies that he or she is the duly elected Secretary of this corporation
and that the above is a true and correct copy of the resolution that was
duly adopted at a meeting of the shareholders which was held in
accordance with state law and the By-Laws of the corporation on
_____ , 19 ___ . I further certify that such resolution is
now in full force and effect.

Dated _____

                                              Seal

_____
Secretary of the corporation

Articles of Dissolution of _____

The undersigned persons, being the holders of all of the issued and outstanding share of stock of this corporation, and being all of the shareholders which are entitled to vote on the dissolution of this corporation in accordance with the By-Laws of this corporation and with the laws of the State of _____ ; do adopt these Articles of Dissolution:

Article 1. The name of the corporation is _____ .

Article 2. The Articles of Incorporation for this corporation were filed with the State of _____ on _____ , 19 ___ .

Article 3. The names and addresses of the directors of this corporation are:

Name   Address

_____   _____

_____   _____

_____   _____

Article 4. The names and addresses of the officers of this corporation are:

Name   Address

_____   _____
President

_____   _____
Vice-President

_____   _____
Secretary

_____   _____
Treasurer

Article 5. The corporation has only one class of stock.

Article 6. A special meeting of the directors of this corporation was held on _____ , 19 ____. At this meeting, a majority of the directors adopted a resolution electing to dissolve this corporation.

Article 7. A special meeting of the shareholders of this corporation was held on _____ , 19 ____. At this meeting, holders of a majority of the shares entitled to vote on the issue of dissolution adopted a resolution electing to dissolve this corporation.

Article 8. This corporation elects to dissolve.

I certify that all of the facts stated in these Articles of Dissolution are true and correct and are made for the purpose of dissolving a business corporation under the laws of the State of _____ .

Dated _____

_____
Secretary of the corporation

Shareholder Name   Signature

_____   _____

_____   _____

_____   _____

_____   _____

_____   _____

_____   _____

_____   _____

Appendix of State Incorporation Information

On the following pages are found state listings containing relevant information regarding incorporation. You are advised to check your state's listing carefully to determine the particular requirements for incorporation in your jurisdiction. Virtually every state has some differing conditions for incorporation. You are also advised to write to the state corporation department for information on incorporation. They will provide you with any necessary updates on the information contained in this Appendix. Following is an explanation of the listings:

State law reference: Should you wish to research the law in your state, this lists the name and chapter of the state statute in which the corporation laws are found in each state.

Title of corporate filing: This listing specifies the name of the document which is filed with the state for incorporation. In this book, it has always been referred to as "Articles of Incorporation". A number of states, however, use different titles. Please substitute the correct title on your form before filing it.

Filing fees: The cost of filing the Articles of Incorporation with the state. In some states, the fee is variable based on the amount of capital stock of the corporation.

Other fees: This listing details any other fees which are due at the time of filing or soon thereafter. These can be franchise taxes, organizational taxes, or various other required fees.

Name reservation: All states allow a proposed corporation to register its corporate name prior to filing in order to reserve the corporation's name. The cost and time limits, however, differ widely.

Name requirements: This listing specifies the corporate designation which is required in each state. Most states allow "corporation", "incorporated", "limited", "company" or some abbreviation of these. However, many states have variations on what designation is allowed.

Incorporator requirements: This designates how many incorporators are required. One is sufficient in most states. This listing also tells whether the incorporators must be persons, or if they can be business entities.

Corporate purpose requirements: This specifies what must be put in the Articles of Incorporation regarding the business purpose of the enterprise. If the listing states: General "all-purpose" clause; you should include the clause which is found in the sample "purpose and powers" clause in Chapter 5. If a specific business purpose is required, replace this general clause with a statement of the actual business purpose.

Director requirements: Most states allow a corporation to have only one director, who may be a non-resident. However, several states have a requirement that the corporation have three directors, unless there are fewer than three shareholders. In these states, if there are less than three shareholders, the number of directors can equal the number of shareholders (ie. a one shareholder corporation can have one director).

Paid-in-capital requirements: Most states have no requirement for paid-in-capital. A few, however, require that the corporation have $1,000 in actual paid-in-capital prior to commencing business. These states also require that you state this fact in the Articles of Incorporation.

Publication requirements: A few states require that you publish either your intention to incorporate or the actual fact of incorporation in a newspaper. Most states, however, do not have this requirement.

Other provisions: This listing details any other special incorporation requirements of each state. These range from additional items which must be added to the Articles of Incorporation to the use of different terminology. Check this listing carefully to determine the situation in your state.

Alabama

Address of State Corporation Department:
Alabama Secretary of State
Alabama Business Division
Post Office Box 5616
Montgomery AL 36103

State law reference: Alabama Business Corporation Act.

Title of corporate filing: Articles of Incorporation.

Filing fees: $40.00 to Secretary of State.

Other fees: Tax: $10 per $1000 of stock (minimum $50); Permit: minimum $10.

Name reservation: Reservable for 120 days for $10.00 fee (required).

Name requirements: Corporation, Incorporated, or abbreviation.

Incorporator requirements: One or more persons, partnerships or corporations.

Corporate purpose requirements: General "all purpose" clause (see instructions).

Director requirements: One or more (may be non-residents).

Paid-in capital requirements: None.

Publication requirements: None.

Other provisions: None.

Alaska

Address of State Corporation Department
Alaska Department of Commerce and Economic Development
Division of Banking, Securities, & Corporations
Post Office Box D
Juneau AK 99801

State law reference: Alaska Statutes, Section 10.06.

Title of corporate filing: Articles of Incorporation.

Filing fees: $150.00.

Other fees: Biennial Corporation Tax at filing: $100.00.

Name reservation: Reservable for 120 days for $ 15.00 fee.

Name requirements: Corporation, Incorporated, Company, Limited, or abbrev.

Incorporator requirements: One or more persons, 18 years or older.

Corporate purpose requirements: General "all purpose" clause (see instructions).

Director requirements: One or more (may be non-residents).

Paid-in capital requirements: None.

Publication requirements: None.

Other provisions: Articles must include a statement of codes from the Alaska Standard Industrial Classification Code List describing business type.

Arizona

Address of State Corporation Department

Arizona Corporation Commission
1200 West Washington
Post Office Box 6019
Phoenix AZ 85005

State law reference: Arizona Revised Statutes, Section 10.

Title of corporate filing: Articles of Incorporation.

Filing fees: $50.00.

Other fees: None.

Name reservation: Reservable for 120 days for $10.00 fee.

Name requirements: Corporation, Incorporated, Company, Limited or abbrev.

Incorporator requirements: Two or more persons.

Corporate purpose requirements: General "all purpose" clause (see instructions).

Director requirements: One or more.

Paid-in capital requirements: None.

Publication requirements: Articles must be published in newspaper 3 times.

Other provisions: Articles must specify ending of corporation's fiscal year.

Arkansas

Address of State Corporation Department

Arkansas Secretary of State
Corporation Department
State Capitol, Room 256
Little Rock AR 72201

State law reference: Arkansas Code, Section 4-27-400+.

Title of corporate filing: Articles of Incorporation.

Filing fees: $50.00.

Other fees: Initial Corporation Franchise Tax due upon filing: minimum $50.

Name reservation: Reservable for 120 days.

Name requirements: Corporation, Incorporated, Company, Limited, or abbrev.

Incorporator requirements: One or more persons.

Corporate purpose requirements: A specific primary purpose must be stated.

Director requirements: One or more (may be non-residents).

Paid-in capital requirements: None.

Publication requirements: None.

Other provisions: There are no preemptive rights unless granted in the Articles.

California

Address of State Corporation Department

    California Secretary of State

    Corporation Division

    1560 Broadway

    Sacramento CA 95814

State law reference: California Corporations Code, Section 200+.

Title of corporate filing: Articles of Incorporation.

Filing fees: $100.

Other fees: Franchise tax upon filing: $800.00; filing agent statement: $5.00.

Name reservation: Reservable for 60 days for $10 fee.

Name requirements: Corporation, Incorporated, Limited, or abbreviation.

Incorporator requirements: One or more persons.

Corporate purpose requirements: General "all purpose" clause (see instructions).

Director requirements: 3 (unless less than 3 shareholders, then same amount).

Paid-in capital requirements: None.

Publication requirements: None.

Other provisions: If initial directors are named in the Articles, they must sign the Articles of Incorporation. No preemptive rights unless granted in Articles.

Colorado

Address of State Corporation Department

    Colorado Secretary of State

    Corporations Section

    1560 Broadway, Suite 200

    Denver CO 80202

State law reference: Colorado Revised Statutes, Section 7-.

Title of corporate filing: Articles of Incorporation.

Filing fees: $50.00.

Other fees: None.

Name reservation: Reservable for 120 days for $10.00 fee (renewable).

Name requirements: Corporation, Incorporated, Company, Limited, or abbrev.

Incorporator requirements: One or more persons, 18 years or older.

Corporate purpose requirements: General "all purpose" clause (see instructions).

Director requirements: 3 (unless less than 3 shareholders, then same amount).

Paid-in capital requirements: None.

Publication requirements: None.

Other provisions: None.

Connecticut

Address of State Corporation Department

Connecticut Secretary of State
Corporation Division
30 Trinity Street
Hartford CT 06115

State law reference: General Statutes of Connecticut, Section 33-.

Title of corporate filing: Certificate of Incorporation.

Filing fees: $45.00.

Other fees: Initial tax upon filing: minimum $150; Initial biennial report: $125.

Name reservation: Reservable for 120 days for a $30.00 fee.

Name requirements: Corporation, Incorporated, Company, Limited, or abbrev.

Incorporator requirements: One or more persons.

Corporate purpose requirements: General "all purpose" clause (see instructions).

Director requirements: 3 (unless less than 3 shareholders, then same amount).

Paid-in capital requirements: Articles must state minimum of $1000.00.

Publication requirements: None.

Other provisions: First corporate report due within 30 days of first organizational meeting.

Delaware

Address of State Corporation Department

Delaware Department of State
Corporation Division
Post Office Box 898
Dover DE 19903

State law reference: Delaware Code, Chapter 1, Title 8.

Title of corporate filing: Certificate of Incorporation.

Filing fees: $25.00.

Other fees: State tax: minimum $15.00.

Name reservation: Reservable for 30 days for $10.00 fee.

Name requirements: Corporation, Incorporated, Company, Limited, or abbrev.

Incorporator requirements: One or more persons, partnerships or corporations.

Corporate purpose requirements: General "all purpose" clause (see instructions).

Director requirements: One or more (may be non-residents).

Paid-in capital requirements: None.

Publication requirements: None.

Other provisions: None.

District of Columbia (Washington D.C.)

Address of State Corporation Department

 Recorder of Deeds
 Superintendent of Corporations
 515 "D" Street
 Washington DC 20001

State law reference: District of Columbia Code, Section 29-.

Title of corporate filing: Articles of Incorporation.

Filing fees: $20.00.

Other fees: Initial License Fee: minimum $20.00; indexing: $2.00.

Name reservation: Reservable for 60 days for $7.00 fee.

Name requirements: Corporation, Incorporated, Company, Limited, or abbrev.

Incorporator requirements: Three or more persons, 18 years or older.

Corporate purpose requirements: A specific primary purpose must be stated.

Director requirements: 3 (unless less than 3 shareholders, then same amount).

Paid-in capital requirements: Articles must state minimum of $1000.00.

Publication requirements: None.

Other provisions: Corporation's name must not indicate that the corporation is organized under an Act of Congress.

Florida

Address of State Corporation Department

 Florida Department of State
 Corporation Division
 Post Office Box 6327
 Tallahassee FL 32304

State law reference: Florida Statutes, Section 607.+

Title of corporate filing: Articles of Incorporation.

Filing fees: $35.00.

Other fees: Registered Agent Designation: $35.00.

Name reservation: Reservable for 120 days for $35.00 fee.

Name requirements: Corporation, Incorporated, Company, or abbreviation.

Incorporator requirements: One or more persons.

Corporate purpose requirements: General "all purpose" clause (see instructions).

Director requirements: One or more (may be non-residents).

Paid-in capital requirements: None.

Publication requirements: None.

Other provisions: A Certificate of Designation of Registered Agent must be filed at the time of filing for incorporation.

Georgia
Address of State Corporation Department
> Georgia Secretary of State
> Corporation Division
> 2 Martin Luther King Drive SE
> Atlanta GA 30334

State law reference: Official Code of Georgia Annotated, Sections 14-2-.
Title of corporate filing: Articles of Incorporation.
Filing fees: $60.
Other fees: Publication of Notice of Intent to file for incorporation: $40.00.
Name reservation: Reservable for 90 days for no fee.
Name requirements: Corporation, Incorporated, Company, Limited, or abbrev.
Incorporator requirements: One or more persons or corporations.
Corporate purpose requirements: General "all purpose" clause (see instructions).
Director requirements: One or more (may be non-residents).
Paid-in capital requirements: None.
Publication requirements: Must publish Notice of Intent to File to incorporate.
Other provisions: None.

Hawaii
Address of State Corporation Department
> Hawaii Department of Commerce and Consumer Affairs
> Business Registration Division
> Post Office Box 40
> Honolulu HI 96813

State law reference: Hawaii Revised Statutes, Section 415-.
Title of corporate filing: Articles of Incorporation.
Filing fees: $50.00.
Other fees: Expedited Service fee: $40.00 (expect long delays without this fee).
Name reservation: Reservable for 120 days.
Name requirements: Corporation, Incorporated, Limited, or abbreviation.
Incorporator requirements: One or more persons or corporations.
Corporate purpose requirements: A specific primary purpose must be stated.
Director requirements: 3 (unless less than 3 shareholders, then same amount).
Paid-in capital requirements: None.
Publication requirements: None.
Other provisions: At least one director must be state resident.

Idaho

Address of State Corporation Department
> Idaho Secretary of State
> Corporation Division
> Statehouse Room 203
> Boise ID 83720

State law reference: Idaho Code, Section 30-.
Title of corporate filing: Articles of Incorporation.
Filing fees: $60.00.
Other fees: None.
Name reservation: Reservable for 4 months for $10.00 fee.
Name requirements: Corporation, Incorporated, Company, Limited, or abbrev.
Incorporator requirements: One or more persons or corporations.
Corporate purpose requirements: A specific primary purpose must be stated.
Director requirements: One or more (may be non-residents).
Paid-in capital requirements: None.
Publication requirements: None.
Other provisions: None.

Illinois

Address of State Corporation Department
> Illinois Secretary of State
> Corporation Division
> Centennial Building, 3rd Floor
> Springfield IL 62756

State law reference: Illinois Annotated Statutes, Chapter 32.
Title of corporate filing: Articles of Incorporation.
Filing fees: $75.00.
Other fees: Initial Franchise Tax: Minimum $25.00.
Name reservation: Reservable for 90 days for $25.00 fee.
Name requirements: Corporation, Incorporated, Company, Limited, or abbrev.
Incorporator requirements: One or more persons or corporations.
Corporate purpose requirements: General "all purpose" clause (see instructions).
Director requirements: One or more (may be non-residents).
Paid-in capital requirements: None.
Publication requirements: None.
Other provisions: Illinois requires the use of state-provided forms for all corporate filings.

Indiana

Address of State Corporation Department

Indiana Secretary of State
Corporation Division
201 State House
Indianapolis IN 46204

State law reference: Indiana Business Corporation Law, Section 23-1-.

Title of corporate filing: Articles of Incorporation.

Filing fees: $90.00.

Other fees: None.

Name reservation: Reservable for 120 days for $20 fee. (Renewable).

Name requirements: Corporation, Incorporated, Company, Limited, or abbrev.

Incorporator requirements: One or more persons.

Corporate purpose requirements: General "all purpose" clause (see instructions).

Director requirements: One or more (may be non-residents).

Paid-in capital requirements: None.

Publication requirements: None.

Other provisions: No preemptive rights unless granted by the Articles of Incorporation.

Iowa

Address of State Corporation Department

Iowa Secretary of State
Corporation Division
Hoover Building, 2nd Floor
Des Moines IA 50319

State law reference: Iowa Code Annotated, Section 493B.

Title of corporate filing: Articles of Incorporation.

Filing fees: $50.00.

Other fees: None.

Name reservation: Reservable for 120 days for $10.00 fee.

Name requirements: Corporation, Incorporated, Company, Limited, or abbrev.

Incorporator requirements: One or more persons or corporations.

Corporate purpose requirements: General "all purpose" clause (see instructions).

Director requirements: One or more (may be non-residents).

Paid-in capital requirements: None.

Publication requirements: None.

Other provisions: No preemptive rights unless granted in the Articles. Names of the initial Board of Directors must be given in the Articles.

Kansas

Address of State Corporation Department
    Kansas Secretary of State
    Corporation Division
    State Capitol, 2nd Floor
    Topeka KS 66612
State law reference: Kansas Statutes Annotated, Section 17-.
Title of corporate filing: Articles of Incorporation.
Filing fees: $75.00.
Other fees: None.
Name reservation: Reservable for 120 days for $20.00 fee.
Name requirements: Many business designation names allowed.
Incorporator requirements: One or more persons, partnerships or corporations.
Corporate purpose requirements: General "all purpose" clause (see instructions).
Director requirements: One or more (may be non-residents).
Paid-in capital requirements: None.
Publication requirements: None.
Other provisions: Names and addresses of initial directors must be given in Articles of Incorporation.

Kentucky

Address of State Corporation Department
    Kentucky Secretary of State
    Corporation Division
    New Capitol Building
    Frankfort KY 40601
State law reference: Kentucky Revised Statutes, Section 271B-.
Title of corporate filing: Articles of Incorporation.
Filing fees: $40.00.
Other fees: Organization Tax: minimum $10.00 (paid to State Treasurer).
Name reservation: Reservable for 120 days for $15.00 fee (renewable).
Name requirements: Corporation, Incorporated, Company, Limited, or abbrev.
Incorporator requirements: One or more persons or corporations.
Corporate purpose requirements: General "all purpose" clause (see instructions).
Director requirements: One or more (may be non-residents).
Paid-in capital requirements: None.
Publication requirements: None.
Other provisions: Number of initial directors must be stated in Articles.

Louisiana

Address of State Corporation Department

Louisiana Secretary of State
Corporation Division
7051 Florida Boulevard
Baton Rouge LA 70804

State law reference: Louisiana Revised Statutes, Section 12:.

Title of corporate filing: Articles of Incorporation.

Filing fees: $60.00.

Other fees: Notary fee in Orleans Parish: $25.00; Recording Articles: variable.

Name reservation: Reservable for 60 days for $20.00 fee.

Name requirements: Corporation, Incorporated, Company, Limited, or abbrev.

Incorporator requirements: One or more persons or corporations.

Corporate purpose requirements: General "all purpose" clause (see instructions).

Director requirements: 3 (unless less than 3 shareholders, then same amount).

Paid-in capital requirements: None.

Publication requirements: None.

Other provisions: Corporate name using "Company" can not be preceded by "and" or "&". No preemptive rights unless granted by Articles.

Maine

Address of State Corporation Department

Maine Secretary of State
Corporation Division
State House Station 101
Augusta ME 04333

State law reference: Maine Revised Statutes, Title 13-A.

Title of corporate filing: Articles of Incorporation.

Filing fees: $75.00.

Other fees: Capital Stock Fee: minimum $30.00.

Name reservation: Reservable for 120 days for $5.00 fee.

Name requirements: No requirements.

Incorporator requirements: One or more persons or corporations.

Corporate purpose requirements: General "all purpose" clause (see instructions).

Director requirements: 3 (unless less than 3 shareholders, then same amount).

Paid-in capital requirements: None.

Publication requirements: None.

Other provisions: Number of initial board of directors must be stated in Articles. Registered Agent is referred to as "Clerk" in Maine.

Maryland

Address of State Corporation Department

Maryland State Department of Assessments and Taxation
Corporation Division
301 West Preston Street, Room 809
Baltimore MD 21201

State law reference: Annotated Code of Maryland, Corp. and Assoc. Articles.

Title of corporate filing: Articles of Incorporation.

Filing fees: $40.00.

Other fees: None.

Name reservation: Reservable for 30 days for $7.00 fee.

Name requirements: Corporation, Incorporated, Company, Limited, or abbrev.

Incorporator requirements: One or more persons.

Corporate purpose requirements: General "all purpose" clause (see instructions).

Director requirements: 3 (unless less than 3 shareholders, then same amount).

Paid-in capital requirements: None.

Publication requirements: None.

Other provisions: If name includes "Company", may not be preceded by "and" or "&". Names of initial directors must be stated in Articles.

Massachusetts

Address of State Corporation Department

Massachusetts Secretary of State
Corporation Division / State House
Boston MA 02133

State law reference: Massachusetts Business Corporation Law, Chapter 156B.

Title of corporate filing: Articles of Organization.

Filing fees: Based on amount of authorized stock: minimum fee $200.00.

Other fees: None.

Name reservation: Reservable for 30 days. Renewable once.

Name requirements: Any name that indicates that business is incorporated.

Incorporator requirements: One or more persons, over 18 years old.

Corporate purpose requirements: A specific primary purpose must be stated.

Director requirements: 3 (unless less than 3 shareholders, then same amount).

Paid-in capital requirements: None.

Publication requirements: None.

Other provisions: Name of initial directors and officers must be stated in Articles of Organization. Secretary is referred to as "clerk" in Massachusetts. End date of fiscal year is required in Articles of Organization.

Michigan

Address of State Corporation Department
Michigan Department of Commerce
Corporation Bureau
Post Office Box 30054
Lansing MI 48926

State law reference: Michigan Compiled Laws, Section 450.
Title of corporate filing: Articles of Incorporation.
Filing fees: $10.00.
Other fees: Organization fee: minimum $50.00.
Name reservation: Reservable for 4 months for $10.00 fee. Renewable.
Name requirements: Corporation, Incorporated, Company, Limited, or abbrev.
Incorporator requirements: One or more persons, partnerships or corporations.
Corporate purpose requirements: General "all purpose" clause (see instructions).
Director requirements: One or more (may be non-residents).
Paid-in capital requirements: None.
Publication requirements: None.
Other provisions: Mandatory filing with Michigan Treasury for various tax licenses is required (sales, use, income withholding, and single business tax).

Minnesota

Address of State Corporation Department
Minnesota Secretary of State
Corporation Division
State Office Building #180
St Paul MN 55155

State law reference: Minnesota Statutes, Section 302A.
Title of corporate filing: Articles of Incorporation.
Filing fees: $135.00.
Other fees: None.
Name reservation: Reservable for 12 months for $35.00 fee. Renewable.
Name requirements: Corporation, Incorporated, Company, Limited, or abbrev.
Incorporator requirements: One or more persons.
Corporate purpose requirements: General "all purpose" clause (see instructions).
Director requirements: One or more.
Paid-in capital requirements: None.
Publication requirements: None.
Other provisions: If name includes "Company", can not be preceded with "and or "&". Cumulative voting allowed unless stated in Articles.

Mississippi

Address of State Corporation Department

Mississippi Secretary of State
Corporation Division
Post Office Box 136
Jackson MS 39205

State law reference: Mississippi Code Annotated, Section 79-4-.

Title of corporate filing: Articles of Incorporation.

Filing fees: $50.00.

Other fees: None.

Name reservation: Reservable for 180 days for $25.00 fee.

Name requirements: Corporation, Incorporated, Company, Limited, or abbrev.

Incorporator requirements: One or more persons.

Corporate purpose requirements: General "all purpose" clause (see instructions).

Director requirements: One or more (may be non-residents).

Paid-in capital requirements: None.

Publication requirements: None.

Other provisions: Initial directors must be named in Articles. Within 60 days of incorporation, must file for Franchise Tax Registration with State Tax Comm.

Missouri

Address of State Corporation Department

Secretary of State
Corporation Division
Post Office Box 778
Jefferson City MO 65102

State law reference: Revised Statutes of Missouri, Section 351.

Title of corporate filing: Articles of Incorporation.

Filing fees: Organization tax: minimum $53.00 based on amount of stock.

Other fees: None.

Name reservation: Reservable for 60 days for $20.00 fee.

Name requirements: Corporation, Incorporated, Company, Limited, or abbrev.

Incorporator requirements: One or more persons, 18 years or older.

Corporate purpose requirements: A specific primary purpose must be stated.

Director requirements: 3 (unless less than 3 shareholders, then same amount).

Paid-in capital requirements: None.

Publication requirements: None.

Other provisions: Number of initial directors must be stated in the Articles of Incorporation.

Montana

Address of State Corporation Department

Montana Secretary of State
Corporation Division
State Capitol
Helena MT 59601

State law reference: Montana Code Annotated, Title 35.

Title of corporate filing: Articles of Incorporation.

Filing fees: $20.00

Other fees: License Fee: minimum $50.00.

Name reservation: Reservable for 120 days for $10.00 fee.

Name requirements: Corporation, Incorporated, Company, Limited, or abbrev.

Incorporator requirements: One or more persons or corporations.

Corporate purpose requirements: General "all purpose" clause (see instructions).

Director requirements: One or more (may be non-residents).

Paid-in capital requirements: None.

Publication requirements: None.

Other provisions: Number of directors must be specified in the Articles of Incorporation.

Nebraska

Address of State Corporation Department

Nebraska Secretary of State
Corporation Division
State Capitol Building, Room 2300
Lincoln NE 68509

State law reference: Revised Statutes of Nebraska, Section 21-.

Title of corporate filing: Articles of Incorporation.

Filing fees: $40.00 minimum: variable fee based on amount of stock.

Other fees: Advertising notice approximately $30.00.

Name reservation: Reservable for 120 days.

Name requirements: Corporation, Incorporated, Company, Limited, or abbrev.

Incorporator requirements: One or more persons.

Corporate purpose requirements: General "all purpose" clause (see instructions).

Director requirements: One or more (may be non-residents).

Paid-in capital requirements: None.

Publication requirements: Notice of incorporation must be published for three consecutive weeks.

Other provisions: None.

Nevada

Address of State Corporation Department
Nevada Secretary of State
Corporation Division
Capitol Complex
Carson City NV 89701

State law reference: Nevada Revised Statutes, Section 78.

Title of corporate filing: Articles of Incorporation.

Filing fees: $125.00 minimum; variable fee based on amount of stock.

Other fees: Filing of list of officers and directors: $85.00.

Name reservation: Reservable for 90 days for $20.00 fee. Non-renewable.

Name requirements: Corporation, Incorporated, Company, Limited, or abbrev.

Incorporator requirements: One or more persons.

Corporate purpose requirements: General "all purpose" clause (see instructions).

Director requirements: One or more (may be non-residents).

Paid-in capital requirements: None.

Publication requirements: None.

Other provisions: No given names may be used in corporate name. A list of officers and directors must be filed with the state.

New Hampshire

Address of State Corporation Department
Department of State
Corporation Division
107 North Main Street
Concord NH 00301

State law reference: New Hampshire Revised Statutes Annotated, Section 293A.

Title of corporate filing: Articles of Incorporation.

Filing fees: $35.00.

Other fees: Filing of Addendum: $50.00; License fee: minimum $75.00-variable.

Name reservation: Reservable for 120 days for $15.00 fee.

Name requirements: Corporation, Incorporated, Limited, or abbreviation.

Incorporator requirements: One or more persons or corporations.

Corporate purpose requirements: A specific primary purpose must be stated.

Director requirements: One or more (may be non-residents).

Paid-in capital requirements: None.

Publication requirements: None.

Other provisions: An Addendum to the Articles must be filed stating that the stock of the corporation is either exempt or has been registered with state.

New Jersey

Address of State Corporation Department
New Jersey Department of State
Corporation Division
C N 308
Trenton NJ 08625

State law reference: New Jersey Statutes, Section 14A.

Title of corporate filing: Certificate of Incorporation.

Filing fees: $100.00.

Other fees: None.

Name reservation: Reservable for 120 days for $50.00 fee.

Name requirements: Corporation, Incorporated, or abbreviation.

Incorporator requirements: One or more persons or corporations.

Corporate purpose requirements: General "all purpose" clause (see instructions).

Director requirements: One or more (may be non-residents).

Paid-in capital requirements: None.

Publication requirements: None.

Other provisions: Number of directors on initial board must be stated in Certificate of Incorporation.

New Mexico

Address of State Corporation Department
New Mexico Secretary of State
Corporation Division
Post Office Box 1269
Santa Fe NM 87504

State law reference: New Mexico Statutes Annotated, Section 53.

Title of corporate filing: Articles of Incorporation.

Filing fees: $50.00; variable fee based on amount of stock.

Other fees: Initial Corporate Report filing fee: $20.00 (filed within 20 days).

Name reservation: Reservable for 120 days for a $10.00 fee.

Name requirements: Corporation, Incorporated, Company, Limited, or abbrev.

Incorporator requirements: One or more persons or corporations.

Corporate purpose requirements: A specific primary purpose must be stated.

Director requirements: One or more (may be non-residents).

Paid-in capital requirements: None.

Publication requirements: None.

Other provisions: None.

New York

Address of State Corporation Department
New York Department of State
Corporation Bureau
162 Washington Street
Albany NY 12231

State law reference: New York Business Corporation Law.
Title of corporate filing: Certificate of Incorporation.
Filing fees: $125.00.
Other fees: Organization tax: minimum $10.00; variable based on stock.
Name reservation: Reservable for 60 days for $20.00 fee. Renewable twice.
Name requirements: Corporation, Incorporated, Limited, or abbreviation.
Incorporator requirements: One or more persons.
Corporate purpose requirements: General "all purpose" clause (but see below).
Director requirements: 3 (unless less than 3 shareholders, then same amount).
Paid-in capital requirements: None.
Publication requirements: None.
Other provisions: Purpose must state corporation needs no approval of any state body. Articles must appoint NY Secretary of State as registered agent.

North Carolina

Address of State Corporation Department
North Carolina Secretary of State
Corporation Division
Capitol Building
Raleigh NC 27603

State law reference: General Statutes of North Carolina, Section 55.
Title of corporate filing: Articles of Incorporation.
Filing fees: $100.00.
Other fees: None.
Name reservation: Reservable for 120 days for $10 fee.
Name requirements: Corporation, Incorporated, Company, Limited, or abbrev.
Incorporator requirements: One or more persons.
Corporate purpose requirements: General "all purpose" clause (see instructions).
Director requirements: One or more (may be non-residents).
Paid-in capital requirements: None.
Publication requirements: None.
Other provisions: None.

North Dakota

Address of State Corporation Department

North Dakota Secretary of State
Corporation Division
Capitol Building
Bismarck ND 58505

State law reference: North Dakota Century Code, Section 10-19.

Title of corporate filing: Articles of Incorporation.

Filing fees: $30.00.

Other fees: Initial Franchise Fee: minimum $50.00; variable (see below also).

Name reservation: Reservable for 12 months for $10.00 fee.

Name requirements: Corporation, Incorporated, Company, Limited, or abbrev.

Incorporator requirements: One or more persons.

Corporate purpose requirements: General "all purpose" clause (see instructions).

Director requirements: One or more.

Paid-in capital requirements: None.

Publication requirements: None.

Other provisions: If "Company" is in corporate name, may not be preceded by "and" or "&". Consent to be Registered Agent must be filed with a $10.00 fee.

Ohio

Address of State Corporation Department

Ohio Secretary of State
Corporation Division
30 East Broad Street
Columbus OH 43266

State law reference: Ohio Revised Code, Section 1701.

Title of corporate filing: Articles of Incorporation.

Filing fees: $75.00 minimum; variable fee based on amount of stock.

Other fees: None.

Name reservation: Reservable for 60 days for $5.00 fee.

Name requirements: Corporation, Incorporated, Company, or abbreviation.

Incorporator requirements: One or more persons.

Corporate purpose requirements: General "all purpose" clause (see instructions).

Director requirements: 3 (unless less than 3 shareholders, then same amount).

Paid-in capital requirements: None.

Publication requirements: None.

Other provisions: Corporate By-Laws are referred to as the corporate "Code of Regulations" in Ohio. Must also file Appointment of Statutory Agent form.

Oklahoma

Address of State Corporation Department

Oklahoma Secretary of State
Corporation Division
101 State Capitol Building
Oklahoma City OK 73105

State law reference: Oklahoma Statutes, Title 18.

Title of corporate filing: Certificate of Incorporation.

Filing fees: $50.00 minimum; variable fee based on amount of stock.

Other fees: None.

Name reservation: Reservable for 60 days for $5.00 fee.

Name requirements: May contain various business designations.

Incorporator requirements: One or more persons, partnerships or corporations.

Corporate purpose requirements: General "all purpose" clause (see instructions).

Director requirements: One or more (may be non-residents).

Paid-in capital requirements: None.

Publication requirements: None.

Other provisions: None.

Oregon

Address of State Corporation Department

Oregon Secretary of State
Corporation Division
158 NE 12th
Salem OR 97310

State law reference: Oregon Business Corporation Act.

Title of corporate filing: Articles of Incorporation.

Filing fees: $50.00.

Other fees: None.

Name reservation: Reservable for 120 days for $10.00 fee.

Name requirements: Corporation, Incorporated, Company, Limited, or abbrev.

Incorporator requirements: One or more persons, partnerships or corporations.

Corporate purpose requirements: General "all purpose" clause (see instructions).

Director requirements: One or more.

Paid-in capital requirements: None.

Publication requirements: None.

Other provisions: None.

Pennsylvania

Address of State Corporation Department
 Pennsylvania Department of State
 Corporation Bureau
 308 North Office Building
 Harrisburg PA 17120

State law reference: Pennsylvania Consolidated Statutes, Section 1300-.
Title of corporate filing: Articles of Incorporation.
Filing fees: $100.00.
Other fees: None.
Name reservation: Reservable for 120 days for $52.00 fee.
Name requirements: May use various business designations.
Incorporator requirements: One or more persons or corporations.
Corporate purpose requirements: General "all purpose" clause (see instructions).
Director requirements: One or more (may be non-residents).
Paid-in capital requirements: None.
Publication requirements: Must publish intent to file or filing of Articles twice.
Other provisions: Must file Docketing Statement at time of filing Articles.

Rhode Island

Address of State Corporation Department
 Rhode Island Secretary of State
 Corporation Division
 100 North Main Street
 Providence RI 20903

State law reference: General Laws of Rhode Island, Section 7-1.
Title of corporate filing: Articles of Incorporation.
Filing fees: $70.00.
Other fees: License Fee: minimum $80.00; variable based on stock amount.
Name reservation: Reservable for 120 days for $50.00 fee.
Name requirements: Corporation, Incorporated, Company, Limited, or abbrev.
Incorporator requirements: One or more persons.
Corporate purpose requirements: A specific primary purpose must be stated.
Director requirements: One or more (may be non-residents).
Paid-in capital requirements: None.
Publication requirements: None.
Other provisions: Registered Agent must sign Articles of Incorporation.

South Carolina

Address of State Corporation Department
> South Carolina Secretary of State
> Corporation Division
> Post Office Box 11350
> Columbia SC 29211

State law reference: Code of Laws of South Carolina, Section 33.

Title of corporate filing: Articles of Incorporation.

Filing fees: $10.00.

Other fees: Incorporation Tax: $100.00; License Fee and Report Fee: $25.00.

Name reservation: Reservable for 120 days for $10.00 fee.

Name requirements: Corporation, Incorporated, Company, Limited, or abbrev.

Incorporator requirements: One or more persons, partnerships or corporations.

Corporate purpose requirements: General "all purpose" clause (see instructions).

Director requirements: One or more (may be non-residents).

Paid-in capital requirements: None.

Publication requirements: None.

Other provisions: Certificate of Attorney must be signed by a South Carolina lawyer. Initial Corporate Report must state specific business purpose.

South Dakota

Address of State Corporation Department
> South Dakota Secretary of State
> Corporation Division
> Capitol Building
> Pierre SD 57501

State law reference: South Dakota Compiled Laws, Section 47.

Title of corporate filing: Articles of Incorporation.

Filing fees: $40.00 minimum; variable fee based on amount of stock.

Other fees: None.

Name reservation: Reservable for 120 days for $10.00 fee.

Name requirements: Corporation, Incorporated, Company, Limited, or abbrev.

Incorporator requirements: One or more persons, 18 years or older.

Corporate purpose requirements: General "all purpose" clause (see instructions).

Director requirements: One or more.

Paid-in capital requirements: Must have paid-in capital of at least $1,000.

Publication requirements: None.

Other provisions: Articles of Incorporation must state number, names and addresses of initial directors.

Tennessee

Address of State Corporation Department

>Tennessee Secretary of State
>Corporation Division
>State Capitol Building
>Nashville TN 37219

State law reference: Tennessee Code Annotated, Section 48.

Title of corporate filing: Certificate of Incorporation.

Filing fees: $50.00.

Other fees: Register of Deeds filing fee: $5.00/page if office is in Tennessee.

Name reservation: Reservable for four months for $10.00 fee.

Name requirements: Corporation, Incorporated, or abbreviation.

Incorporator requirements: One or more persons, partnerships or corporations.

Corporate purpose requirements: General "all purpose" clause (see instructions).

Director requirements: One or more (may be non-residents).

Paid-in capital requirements: None.

Publication requirements: None.

Other provisions: Certificate of Incorporation also referred to as the Corporate Charter in Tennessee.

Texas

Address of State Corporation Department

>Texas Secretary of State
>Corporation Section
>Post Office Box 13697
>Austin TX 78711

State law reference: Texas Business Corporation Act.

Title of corporate filing: Articles of Incorporation.

Filing fees: $300.00.

Other fees: Initial Franchise Tax: $100.00.

Name reservation: Reservable for 120 days for $40.00 fee.

Name requirements: Corporation, Incorporated, or abbreviation.

Incorporator requirements: One or more persons, partnerships or corporations.

Corporate purpose requirements: General "all purpose" clause (see instructions).

Director requirements: One or more (may be non-residents).

Paid-in capital requirements: Paid-in capital must be at least $1,000.

Publication requirements: Notice must be published if an operating company intends to incorporate without changing the firm's name.

Other provisions: Number, names and addresses of initial directors in Articles.

Utah

Address of State Corporation Department
> Utah Secretary of State
> Division of Corporations and Commercial Code
> Post Office Box 45801
> Salt Lake City UT 84103

State law reference: Utah Code Annotated, Section 16-10.
Title of corporate filing: Articles of Incorporation.
Filing fees: $50.00.
Other fees: None.
Name reservation: Reservable for 120 days for $20.00 fee.
Name requirements: Corporation, Incorporated, Company, or abbreviation.
Incorporator requirements: Three or more persons, 18 years or older.
Corporate purpose requirements: A specific primary purpose must be stated.
Director requirements: 3 (unless less than 3 shareholders, then same amount).
Paid-in capital requirements: Must have at least $1,000 of paid-in capital.
Publication requirements: None.
Other provisions: Names and addresses of the initial directors must be stated in the Articles of Incorporation. Registered Agent must sign Articles.

Vermont

Address of State Corporation Department
> Vermont Secretary of State
> Corporation Division
> 109 State Street
> Montpelier VT 05602

State law reference: Vermont Statutes Annotated, Title 11.
Title of corporate filing: Articles of Association.
Filing fees: $35.00 minimum; variable fee based on amount of stock.
Other fees: None.
Name reservation: Reservable for 120 days for $10.00 fee.
Name requirements: Corporation, Incorporated, Company, Limited, or abbrev.
Incorporator requirements: One or more persons, 18 years or older.
Corporate purpose requirements: A specific primary purpose must be stated.
Director requirements: 3 (unless less than 3 shareholders, then same amount).
Paid-in capital requirements: None.
Publication requirements: None.
Other provisions: Number, names and addresses of the initial directors must be stated in the Articles of Association.

Virginia

Address of State Corporation Department
> Virginia State Corporation Commission
> 1220 Bank Street
> Post Office Box 1197
> Richmond VA 23219

State law reference: Code of Virginia, Title 13.1.
Title of corporate filing: Articles of Incorporation.
Filing fees: $25.00.
Other fees: Charter fee: $50.00 minimum; variable fee based on stock amount.
Name reservation: Reservable for 120 days for $10.00 fee.
Name requirements: Corporation, Incorporated, Company, Limited, or abbrev.
Incorporator requirements: One or more persons.
Corporate purpose requirements: General "all purpose" clause (see instructions).
Director requirements: One or more (may be non-residents).
Paid-in capital requirements: None.
Publication requirements: None.
Other provisions: None.

Washington

Address of State Corporation Department
> Washington Secretary of State
> Corporation Division
> 505 East Union Street
> Olympia WA 98504

State law reference: Revised Code of Washington, Title 23-B.
Title of corporate filing: Articles of Incorporation.
Filing fees: $175.00.
Other fees: Annual Report filing: $10.00 (file within 120 days of incorporation).
Name reservation: Reservable for 180 days for $20.00 fee.
Name requirements: Corporation, Incorporated, Company, Limited, or abbrev.
Incorporator requirements: One or more persons or corporations.
Corporate purpose requirements: General "all purpose" clause (see instructions).
Director requirements: One or more (may be non-residents).
Paid-in capital requirements: None.
Publication requirements: None.
Other provisions: Must state official Washington State Unified Business Identifier in Articles, if issued. Registered Agent must sign Articles.

West Virginia

Address of State Corporation Department

West Virginia Secretary of State
Corporation Division
State Capitol Building
Charleston WV 25305

State law reference: West Virginia Code, Chapter 31, Article 1.

Title of corporate filing: Articles of Incorporation.

Filing fees: $10.00.

Other fees: Annual license tax: $75 minimum; variable fee based on stock.

Name reservation: Reservable for 120 days for a $5.00 fee.

Name requirements: Corporation, Incorporated, Company, Limited, or abbrev.

Incorporator requirements: One or more persons or corporations.

Corporate purpose requirements: General "all purpose" clause (see instructions).

Director requirements: One or more (may be non-residents).

Paid-in capital requirements: None.

Publication requirements: None.

Other provisions: Number of initial directors must be stated in the Articles of Incorporation.

Wisconsin

Address of State Corporation Department

Wisconsin Secretary of State
Corporation Division
Post Office Box 7846
Madison WI 53701

State law reference: Wisconsin Statutes Annotated, Section 180.

Title of corporate filing: Articles of Incorporation.

Filing fees: $90.00 minimum; variable fee based on amount of stock.

Other fees: None.

Name reservation: Reservable for 120 days for $15.00 fee.

Name requirements: Corporation, Incorporated, Company, Limited, or abbrev.

Incorporator requirements: One or more persons.

Corporate purpose requirements: General "all purpose" clause (see instructions).

Director requirements: One or more (may be non-residents).

Paid-in capital requirements: None.

Publication requirements: None.

Other provisions: None.

Wyoming

Address of State Corporation Department
> Wyoming Secretary of State
> Corporation Division
> State Capitol Building
> Cheyenne WY 82002

State law reference: Wyoming Statutes, Section 17-16.

Title of corporate filing: Articles of Incorporation.

Filing fees: $90.00 ($30.00 credit if filed when reserving name).

Other fees: None.

Name reservation: Reservable for 120 days for $30.00 fee.

Name requirements: Corporation, Incorporated, or abbreviation.

Incorporator requirements: One or more persons or corporations.

Corporate purpose requirements: A specific primary purpose must be stated.

Director requirements: One or more (may be non-residents).

Paid-in capital requirements: None.

Publication requirements: None.

Other provisions: Written Consent to Appointment as Registered Agent must accompany filing of Articles of Incorporation.

Glossary of Corporate Legal Terms

Agent: A person who is authorized to act on behalf of another. A corporation acts only through its agents, whether they are directors, employees, or officers.

Articles of Incorporation: The charter of the corporation, this is the public filing with a state which requests that the corporation be allowed to exist. Along with the corporate By-Laws, it provides details of the organization and structure of the business. They must be consistent with the laws of the state of incorporation.

Assumed name: A name, other than the corporation's legal name as shown on the Articles of Incorporation, under which a corporation will conduct business. Most states require registration of the fictitious name if a company desires to conduct business under an assumed name. The corporation's legal name is not an assumed name.

Authorized stock: The number of shares of stock that a corporation is allowed to issue as stated in the Articles of Incorporation. All authorized shares need not be issued.

Board of directors: The group with control of the general supervision of the corporation. They are elected by the shareholders and they, in turn, appoint the officers of the corporation.

Business corporation laws: For each individual state, these provide the legal framework for the operation of corporations. The Articles of Incorporation and the By-Laws of a corporation must adhere to the specifics of state law.

By-Laws: The internal rules which govern the management of the corporation. They contain the procedures for holding meetings, appointments, elections and other management matters. If these conflict with the Articles of Incorporation, the provision in the Articles will be controlling.

Capital: Initially, the actual money or property that shareholders transfer to the corporation to allow it to operate. Once in operation, it also consists of accumulated profits. The net worth of the corporation.

Capital stock: See *Authorized stock*.

Certificate of Incorporation: See *Articles of Incorporation*. Note, however, some states will issue a Certificate of Incorporation after the filing of the Articles of Incorporation.

Close corporation: Corporation with less than 50 shareholders and which has elected to be treated as a close corporation. Not all states have close corporation statutes. (For information regarding close corporations, please consult a competent attorney).

Closely-held corporation: Not a specific state-sanctioned type of corporation, but rather a designation of any corporation in which the stock is held by a small group of people or entities and is not publicly traded.

Common stock: The standard stock of a corporation which includes the right to vote the shares and the right to proportionate dividends. See also *Preferred stock*.

Consent Resolution: Any resolution signed by all of the directors or shareholders of a corporation authorizing an action, without the necessity of a meeting.

Cumulative voting: A voting right of shareholders which allows votes for directors to be spread among the various nominees. This right protects the voting strength of minority shareholders. The amount of votes in cumulative voting is based on the number of shares held times the number of director positions to be voted on. The shareholder can then allocate the total cumulative votes in any manner.

Dissolution: Methods by which a corporation concludes its business and liquidates. Dissolutions may be involuntary because of bankruptcy or credit problems or voluntary on the initiation of the directors or shareholders of a corporation.

Dividend: A distribution of money or property paid by the corporation to a shareholder based on the amount of shares held. Dividends must be paid out of the corporations net earnings and profits. The board of directors has the authority to declare or withhold dividends based on sound business discretion.

Domestic corporation: A corporation is a domestic corporation in the state in which it is incorporated. See also *Foreign corporation*.

Fictitious name: See *Assumed name*.

Foreign corporation: A corporation is referred to as a foreign corporation in all states other than the one in which it is actually incorporated. In order to conduct active business affairs in a different state, foreign corporation must be registered with the other state for the authority to transact business and it must pay an annual fee for this privilege.

Incorporator: The person who signs the Articles of Incorporation. Usually a person, but some states allow a corporation or partnership to be an incorporator.

Indemnify: To reimburse or compensate. Directors and officers of corporations are often reimbursed or indemnified for all the expenses they may have incurred in incorporating.

Issued shares: The number of authorized shares of stock that are actually transferred to shareholders of the corporation. Also referred to as outstanding shares. See also *Treasury shares*.

Minutes: A written record of the activities of a meeting.

No-par value: Shares of stock which have no specific face value. The board of directors can assign a value to the shares for sale and can then allocate a portion of the sales price to the paid-in-capital account.

Not-for-profit corporation: A corporation formed under state law which exists for a socially-worthwhile purpose. Profits are not distributed but retained and used for corporate purposes. May be tax-exempt. Also referred to as non-profit.

Officers: Manage the daily operations of a corporation. Generally consists of a president, vice-president, secretary, and treasurer. Appointed by the board of directors.

Par value: The face value assigned to shares of stock. Par value stock must be sold for at least the stated value, but can be sold for more than the par value.

Piercing the corporate veil: A legal decision that allows a court to ignore the corporate entity and reach the assets of the shareholders, directors, or officers.

Preemptive rights: A shareholder right that allows shareholders the opportunity to maintain their percentage of ownership of the corporation in the event that additional shares are offered for sale.

Preferred stock: Generally, stock which provides the shareholder with a preferential payment of dividends, but does not carry voting rights.

Proxy: A written shareholder authorization to vote shares on behalf of another. Directors may never vote by proxy (except in some close corporations).

Quorum: The required number of persons necessary to officially conduct business at a meeting. Generally, a majority of the shareholders or directors constitutes a quorum.

Registered agent: The person designated in the Articles of Incorporation who will be available to receive service of process (summons, subpoena, etc.) on behalf of the corporation. A corporation must always have a registered agent.

Registered office: The actual physical location of the registered agent. Need not be the actual principal place of business of the corporation.

Resolutions: A formal decision which has been adopted by either the shareholders or the board of directors of a corporation.

"S" corporation: A specific IRS designation which allows a corporation to be taxed similarly to a partnership, yet retain limited liability for its shareholders.

Shareholders: Own issued stock of a corporation and, therefore, own an interest in the corporation. They elect the board of directors and vote on major corporate issues.

Stock transfer book: The ledger book (or sheets) in which the registered owners of shares in the corporation are recorded.

Treasury shares: Shares of stock which were issued, but later re-acquired by the corporation and not cancelled. May be issued as dividends to shareholders. They are issued but not outstanding for terms of voting and quorums.

Index

251

Nova Publishing Company

The Finest in Small Business and Consumer Legal Books